Christian Safran

Social Media in Education

Christian Safran

Social Media in Education

Application Scenarios in the Context of Technology-Enhanced Learning at Universities

Südwestdeutscher Verlag für Hochschulschriften

Impressum/Imprint (nur für Deutschland/ only for Germany)

Bibliografische Information der Deutschen Nationalbibliothek: Die Deutsche Nationalbibliothek verzeichnet diese Publikation in der Deutschen Nationalbibliografie; detaillierte bibliografische Daten sind im Internet über http://dnb.d-nb.de abrufbar.

Alle in diesem Buch genannten Marken und Produktnamen unterliegen warenzeichen-, marken- oder patentrechtlichem Schutz bzw. sind Warenzeichen oder eingetragene Warenzeichen der jeweiligen Inhaber. Die Wiedergabe von Marken, Produktnamen, Gebrauchsnamen, Handelsnamen, Warenbezeichnungen u.s.w. in diesem Werk berechtigt auch ohne besondere Kennzeichnung nicht zu der Annahme, dass solche Namen im Sinne der Warenzeichen- und Markenschutzgesetzgebung als frei zu betrachten wären und daher von jedermann benutzt werden dürften.

Verlag: Südwestdeutscher Verlag für Hochschulschriften Aktiengesellschaft & Co. KG
Dudweiler Landstr. 99, 66123 Saarbrücken, Deutschland
Telefon +49 681 37 20 271-1, Telefax +49 681 37 20 271-0
Email: info@svh-verlag.de
Zugl.: Graz, TU, Diss., 2010

Herstellung in Deutschland:
Schaltungsdienst Lange o.H.G., Berlin
Books on Demand GmbH, Norderstedt
Reha GmbH, Saarbrücken
Amazon Distribution GmbH, Leipzig
ISBN: 978-3-8381-1645-7

Imprint (only for USA, GB)

Bibliographic information published by the Deutsche Nationalbibliothek: The Deutsche Nationalbibliothek lists this publication in the Deutsche Nationalbibliografie; detailed bibliographic data are available in the Internet at http://dnb.d-nb.de.

Any brand names and product names mentioned in this book are subject to trademark, brand or patent protection and are trademarks or registered trademarks of their respective holders. The use of brand names, product names, common names, trade names, product descriptions etc. even without a particular marking in this works is in no way to be construed to mean that such names may be regarded as unrestricted in respect of trademark and brand protection legislation and could thus be used by anyone.

Publisher: Südwestdeutscher Verlag für Hochschulschriften Aktiengesellschaft & Co. KG
Dudweiler Landstr. 99, 66123 Saarbrücken, Germany
Phone +49 681 37 20 271-1, Fax +49 681 37 20 271-0
Email: info@svh-verlag.de

Printed in the U.S.A.
Printed in the U.K. by (see last page)
ISBN: 978-3-8381-1645-7

Contents

Chapter 1 Introduction

"Tell me and I forget. Show me and I remember. Involve me and I understand."

(Chinese proverb)

For years *e-learning* and *technology-enhanced learning* had been focused on supporting the formal aspects of learning by providing predefined structures and learning material. Yet informal learning, which is unconscious learning not based on curricula and exams, has always been part of human nature, and, to some extent, part of education. Considered within the learning process, it can be used to support and enhance the learning progress. Social media, with their possibilities to communicate, reflect, and collaborate, provide means of supporting informal learning in *e-learning* and *technology-enhanced learning*.

1.1 Motivation

In 2006, the year when the research work recapitulated in this book began, Time Magazine[1] made an unforeseen step when announcing the *Person of the Year*. Instead of assigning this award to a single person, it was assigned to *you*. It was assigned to the people who were responsible for the success and the innovations associated with the "new Web", the so-called *Web 2.0* [Grossman, 2006].

This, at that time massively popular, meme fails to completely describe the changes which the World Wide Web had seen in those years, and which have continued in the three years until that time. These changes are not predominately based on technology, as the technology applied has already been known for several years, but are changes in the way people interact with this technology and with each other. As such, *Web 2.0* does not describe some concrete technology, but rather presents a concept, which

---

[1] http://www.time.com/, accessed 2009-09-03

summarizes a set of technological and sociological developments. These developments are based on participation and a revolutionary movement towards the freedom of information [Möller, 2006].

Web 2.0, Read-Write-Web, Social Web – several terms can be used to describe these developments which are centered on the shift from the Web as a place of *producers* and *consumers* of content to a place of *communities*, where everyone can publish information, and which is a place for the users to interconnect, communicate, collaborate and share. As such, these developments bring the Web closer to the place it had originally been envisioned by Sir Tim Berners-Lee [Anderson, 2006].

Social media are one aspect of this concept encompassing the technologies and principles for the publication of user generated content. "Social media essentially is a category of online media where people are talking, participating, sharing, networking, and bookmarking online. Most social media services encourage discussion, feedback, voting, comments, and sharing of information from all interested parties." [Jones, 2009]

Not too long after Web 2.0 had made its appearance in public perception, the ideas involved started to influence e-learning, as well as technology-enhanced learning. E-learning, which is based on supporting the learning process via ICT, was especially well prepared for this development, since community tools, like discussion forums and instant messaging, had been prominently featured in e-learning systems for quite some time. Yet, also in technology-enhanced learning and teaching, which also encompasses classroom education, the trend towards the inclusion of informal learning scenarios was well received. These informal learning scenarios can greatly benefit from the support of technologies associated with Web 2.0 [Granitzer et al., 2008].

This book aims to provide the reader with an introduction to the intersection of the *Social Web* and *technology-enhanced learning*, with a focus on learning in higher education settings. It offers a sound description of selected application scenarios for social media in the context of supporting individual learners and, most of all, learning communities in their knowledge acquisition. These scenarios cover several of the better-known technologies of social media and their application to higher education.

1.2 Research Scope

It has been suggested that social media have enormous potential impact on e-learning and technology-enhanced learning, especially in the context of contemporary learning styles [Baird and Fisher, 2006]. This impact is only partially technologically based. As with the concept of Web 2.0 as a whole, the effects on learning are technical as well as social in character. They encompass the strong integration of informal scenarios, the motivation to engage with the learning targets outside a classroom situation.

Social media include technologies like wikis, weblogs, and instant messaging, which enable users to publish and collaborate and form online communities [Schaffert, 2006]. In contrast to classic media, the publication of content is straightforward and inexpensive. Moreover, social media are based on the notion of connecting users, as well as forming and supporting communities.

This book focuses primarily on the application of social media to teaching and learning in higher education. In the context of the Web, the promotion of social media marked the shift of *producer-generated content* towards *user-generated content*. In the context of technology-enhanced learning, this paradigm change marks the shift from classic e-learning, based on courses and the (sequential) presentation of learning material, towards a more active participation of the learners and the support of the learners as a community of interest.

As such, social media are predestinated to support traditional learning, as well as e-learning approaches. This is achieved by fostering informal learning in addition to formal learning, which typically occurs in university curricula. The recognition of informal learning parallels the shift in pedagogical paradigms from behaviorism to cognitivism and to constructivism. Informal learning, with its ongoing characteristic, is even more valuable outside the traditional education, like i.e. in workplace-integrated learning, where information is permanently sought and provided [Tochermann and Granitzer, 2008].

1.3 Research Questions & Results

The research presented in this book focuses on the design, development, implementation and evaluation of application scenarios for social media in the context of (higher) education. These application scenarios have been selected in order to answer the subsequently listed research questions. The corresponding results are briefly summarized for each research question.

Are the students familiar with the applications and technologies summarized under the term Web 2.0? This very basic research question was answered by a set of surveys conducted during the period from 2006 to 2009. Based on an initial survey in 2006, the initial status at the beginning of this research was identified. Students had a high level of familiarity with the better-known applications of Web 2.0, but lacked knowledge about more recent trends. Moreover, only a minority of the students was actively publishing content in Web 2.0.

Are students using social media tools for learning? Are they confronted with such tools in the lectures? This research question was likewise answered with surveys conducted among the students. Leaving aside wikis, the students had very little contact with social media tools in the context of education.

How can the concepts of e-learning 2.0 be applied to computer science (specifically software development) education? As the answer to the previous research question had shown that the students already used wikis, the further research on this question was focused on the application of weblogs as the second core application to the context of e-learning 2.0. An application scenario for weblogs as learning logs in software development education was developed. The applicability of quantitative measurements for the prediction of overall learning performance was verified.

How can social media concepts be applied to enhance self-reflection and feedback from the community? The concept of peer review has been adapted to improve software development education and extended by collaborative online features in order to foster critical engagement with the own work and the work of peers.

How can social media concepts be applied to aid the externalization of knowledge in a community of learners? In this context, a well-known technology for brainstorming and visualization of knowledge has been adapted to a social media application by developing a collaborative online mind-mapping tool. Possible application scenarios for education have been formulated and evaluated.

How can social media be applied to the context of mobile learning in higher education? Location based services have seen a renaissance in the last years due to possibilities mashups with readily available mapping material provide. In this context, a collaborative, lightweight, and location-based collaborative system has been developed to support excursions in higher education.

1.4 Methodology and Structure

The methodology applied to the research presented in this book is based on the notions of *scenarios* and *services* defined to itemize the manifold topic of social media to solve concrete problems and enhance learning in concrete situations.

1.4.1 Scenarios

"Scenarios are devices for improving our perception". A problem becomes cognitively manageable and can better be memorized by putting a complex set of events and relationships into a story. [Van der Heijden, 1997]

A scenario is an "idealized but detailed description" of a specific situation [Young and Barnard, 1987]. Moreover, a scenario is an informal methodology widely used in requirement engineering [Alspaugh and Antón, 2008]. One of the main advantages is the encouragement of the designer to envision outcomes before attempting to specify them, making requirements more proactive in the development [Carroll et al., 1998].

Scenarios can be used to identify details of individual research questions. Moreover, they can be used to develop evaluation scenarios for individual research goals. As far as education is concerned, the OECD[2] encourages the definition of scenarios for the research of future education in order to provide a basis for stakeholders from various fields in order to develop long-term strategies [OECD Publishing, 2006].

In technology-enhanced learning, scenarios are used in the context of an activity-based didactical theory. Within this didactical model, learning scenarios are defined as a sequence of activities, a list of involved user roles, the applied system tools, and the educational content [Helic, 2005]. These scenarios provide the fundamental organization of the learning process within this approach.

In the context of this research, scenarios were used firstly to describe the individual problem domains for selected aspects of social media to be applied to education and thus, by offering concrete situations, clarify the possible impact on the learning process. Secondly, these scenarios define a set of test cases with which the proposed solution can be evaluated to verify the validity of the approach. This methodological approach resulted in structuring this book as described below.

1.4.2 Independent Services vs. Monolithic Multipurpose Systems

The second pillar of the research presented in this book is the focus on individual services rather than the design of a monolithic system, mirroring the *Web 2.0* development principles in the context of *web services*. A web service is "a software system designed to support interoperable machine-to-machine interaction over a

---

[2] Organisation for Economic Co-operation and Development

network. It has an interface described in a machine-processable format (specifically WSDL[3])" [W3C Working Group, 2004].

Among the core characteristics of Web services are *loose coupling* and *composition* [Bettag, 2001]. The term *loose coupling* describes the fact that communication with web services is conducted via messages. The details of the implementation of the web service remain hidden, only the messages are specified. *Composition* denotes the fact that web services can be rearranged or integrated into superordinate services. It encourages developers to design web services primarily for atomic tasks and implement systems that are more complex by using these individual services.

The advantage of the principles used in the development of web services is their potential *simplicity* [O'Reilly, 2005]. Although initially large companies had developed complex, oversized web service stacks, these approaches failed to be widely used. In contrast, simplistic approaches like the Google Maps API[4] have been welcomed by Web developers with open arms. This simplicity is achieved by easy access, as well as the fact that these web services are specialized on a restricted set of tasks.

Simplicity offers the additional benefit of encouraging *mashups* of existing services, to provide new, innovative solutions. A mashup "is a website or web application that seamlessly combines content from more than one source into an integrated experience" [Jackson and Wang, 2007]. By using existing, specialized services, development resources can be used on new and alternative applications. Maybe the best example of successful mashups is the vast number of applications making use of the Google Maps API in order to display location based information on a map. Without the provision of such high quality mapping material, the same information would be less significant.

---

[3] Web Service Description Language
[4] http://code.google.com/intl/en/apis/maps/, accessed 2009-08-27

In the research presented in this book, the same approach was chosen. Instead of defining a monolithic system providing a vast set of possible social media concepts for education, a set of independent solutions for the previously defined research questions and scenarios has been developed. These solutions are either mashups on their own, or provide themselves access to external applications in order to be used in other mashups.

1.4.3 Structure

The remainder of this book is structured into two main parts. The first part focuses on the research background and the general application of social media to technology-enhanced learning. It commences with an introduction into the domain of social media in general and two prominent examples, weblogs and wikis, in particular. Moreover, an overview of e-learning and technology-enhanced learning and the transition from "classic" e-learning to e-learning 2.0 is given. Part I closes with a detailed analysis of the status quo of social media in higher education at the beginning of the research covered in this book. The analysis focuses on Graz University of Technology and takes into account both the knowledge of the students about social media and other Web tools, as well as the application of such tools in teaching and learning at our university.

Subsequently, the second part of this book discusses four scenarios for the application of the theoretical concepts discussed in part I. All of the described application scenarios are set in the domain of technology-enhanced learning in higher education.

1.4.4 Scenario 1: Learning by Self-Reflection

In the next chapter, the first scenario of a social media application is presented as a solution to the second research question formulated above. Learning logs have already been used in education for quite some time [Baker, 2003]. They follow the basic notion of providing an incentive for self-reflection and deeper engagement with a topic. Weblogs (blogs), with their basic intention of providing an easy to use possibility of publishing a "diary" online, provide the Web 2.0 application ideally suited for the support of the learning log concept in an online context.

The social aspect of weblogs becomes obvious through the communication of the authors of individual blogs, either via comments on the entries or by citations and so-called trackbacks (see 2.1.1). This communication and discussion among the individual learners, as well as the learners and the teachers, offers an additional benefit as opposed to offline learning logs.

This scenario is set in the context of university software development education. A lecturer provides his students with the arbitrary possibility to write their own weblogs to log their advances in the practical examples, post questions or problems, and discuss general notions connected with the topic of the lecture. These weblogs can be accessed by all students participating in the lecture, as well as the lecturer, and tutors, who are responsible for the supervision of individual groups of students.

Chapter 5 presents the realization of this scenario in a first-year programming lecture and an evaluation of the usefulness of this approach. This evaluation contains an analysis of the correlation of the weblogs with the learning performance, as well as well as an analysis of the possible use of quantitative measures as predictors for the lecture performance in general.

1.4.5 Scenario 2: Peer Review in Software Development Education

The next scenario addresses the third research question of possible transfer of technology-enhanced learning concepts into the domain of the Social Web. Peer review is a technique used in the context of education to extend the feedback given to the individual learners. As opposed to feedback from a single source (the teacher), the learners are given additional feedback by their peers. Moreover, for the individual reviewers, the peer review offers a possibility to enhance their own ability to give feedback, and to gain additional insights on a topic by seeing alternative approaches. Finally, by adding the element of rating the peers' work, peer review can be integrated into the grading as peer assessment.

Peer review itself is based on the communication of reviewer and original author, albeit restricted to a single direction. In order to enhance this approach this communication can be improved to be bidirectional and thus allow the original author to comment on the review. Moreover, a possibility can be provided for the peers to collaborate on the review and thus improve its quality.

This scenario again is set in the context of a university software development lecture. Due to a high number of participants, the individual learners usually work in groups. Thus, the learners receive little feedback for their individual parts of the exercise, and are mainly supported regarding their group exercise. Peer review can be used to offer additional feedback on small, individual examples. Subsequent peer rating can even into the grading of the lecture as peer assessment, if precautions on the quality of this rating are taken.

Chapter 6 presents the implementation of a Web based peer review application to support this scenario. It takes into account the "professional" feedback of tutors as well as the peers' feedback through peer review, and offers a mechanism to judge a facultative rating of the programming examples for suitability to be integrated in the lecture grading. An evaluation explores the learners' reaction to this application and the quality of their reviews and rating.

1.4.6 Scenario 3: Collaborative Brainstorming

The following scenario presents yet another technique transferred to the context of the Social Web. Mind-mapping is a method of capturing and structure knowledge into a two-dimensional, structured visualization. In learning and teaching, these maps can be beneficial due to the fact that cognitive processes can be enhanced, if they are exteriorized and visualized [Jonassen, 1992].

Mind-mapping can be transferred into the context of Social Web by adding collaborative features to an online mind-mapping tool. This collaboration can be useful in a synchronous as well as an asynchronous scenario and must support the possibility to merge individual work into one collaborative mind map.

This scenario once again is set in the context of university software development education. A lecturer wants to offer students a tool to collaboratively brainstorm and model the requirements of the programming examples in order to improve their understanding of the "user wish" regarding the developed software. These considerations should be made before the actual software design process, and as such, a mind-map can be perceived as a more appropriate method than UML diagrams, which are to be concluded later on.

Chapter 7 presents the implementation of a collaborative online mind-mapping tool for higher education, which can be applied to this scenario. Moreover, several application scenarios of collaborative online mind-mapping in higher education are discussed. Finally, an evaluation of the usefulness and a comparison with concept-mapping is provided.

1.4.7 Scenario 4: Collaborative Learning in Location-Related Fields

Finally, the last scenario presented addresses the support for those curricula in higher education, which are dealing with location-based information and learning. Typical examples are civil engineering, architecture, archeology, and geo-sciences. One part of education in these fields is learning *on-site* in field trips and excursions.

Such fields of education can profit greatly from mobile learning (m-learning) based on the actual locations visited. As such, the addition of location information to digital resources (geotagging) is an important issue in this context. Moreover, m-learning can further be improved by adding collaborative work in order to address and support the informal character of learning in-the-field.

This scenario is set in the context of learning in-the-field, and suitable for all fields of study, which involve excursions. A lecturer wants to provide a tool that supports all three phases of an excursion: the preparation, the field trip, and the review. Especially in the field, a mobile and lightweight solution must be available. The students should be encouraged to learn collaboratively in all of the phases, and most of the information involved is location-based.

Chapter 8 presents the development of a specialized geospatial wiki designed to provide a unique combination of collaborative learning, geotagged information, and a mobile application. This application is based on the notion of information entities called *places*, which correspond real-world *locations* and form the individual articles (or *pages*) in the wiki. Moreover, several alternative application scenarios for this geospatial wiki are presented, as well as the evaluation of some of these. Finally, an approach for the introduction of the microblog paradigm into this wiki application in order to provide an easy method for a geotagged information-push is presented.

1.5 Scientific Contributions

This book covers the results of more than three years of research (2006-2009). Some parts of this work are based on research which has partly already been published, as author or co-author, in peer-reviewed conference proceedings, book chapters and journals:

- [Kolbitsch et al., 2007]
- [Maurer and Safran, 2007]
- [Safran and Kappe, 2007]
- [Safran and Kappe, 2008]
- [Safran and Zaka, 2008]
- [Safran et al., 2007a]
- [Safran et al., 2007b]
- [Safran et al., 2009a]
- [Safran et al., 2009b]
- [Safran et al., 2009c]
- [Safran, 2008a]
- [Safran, 2008b]
- [Safran, 2009a]
- [Safran, 2009b]
- [Zaka and Safran, 2008]

PART I

The Two Pillars: Social Media and Technology-Enhanced Learning

Chapter 2 Social Media

The remainder of this book will, from a technological point of view, be deeply focused on the major part of the phenomenon of *Web 2.0*. *Social media* describes the creation of (online) content by users (or communities) as opposed to classic media, which rely on publishers. Social media are characterized by participation, openness, conversation, connectedness and sense of communality [Mayfield, 2008]. From this definition, three core aspects can be identified to converge into social media: communication, collaboration, and sharing.

The term *social media* is sometimes used synonymously with *social software*. However, *social media* are always used in the context of publication or creation of content, either for a closed or open form of community of interest. *Social software*, in contrast, is a general term describing software systems supporting communication and collaboration, and thus the term includes several applications which cannot be identified as social media, e.g. instant messaging. [Bächle, 2006]

This chapter commences with a closer look at these concepts and presents the Web technologies applied to this context. Finally, a closer look is taken on two selected applications of social web, weblogs and online collaborative systems. For weblogs, the question why some weblogs are more successful than others is investigated. As far as collaborative systems are concerned, possibilities beyond the probably best-known collaborative system, Wikipedia, are presented.

2.1 Social Media Concepts

Within this book the concept of *social media* is defined by the application of one or more of the three subordinate concepts communication, collaboration and sharing. Furthermore, for each of these concepts several types of Web applications can be identified as representative. Each of these exemplary applications, in turn, brings a connection to the *Social Web*.

2.1.1 Communication

Probably the most vital aspect of *social media* is *communication* in the form of *computer-mediated communication*. Computer-mediated communication has been shown to be comparable in sociality to face-to-face communication, at least at the group level [Watt et al., 2002]. In the context of social media, and thus the publication of content within online communities, this communication on group level is of special interest. Thus, direct communication between individuals, e.g. with instant messaging, is not taken into account within this chapter.

2.1.1.1 Discussion Forums

Discussion forums are probably the earliest form of social software which could also be considered a medium. It is an asynchronous, interactive form of communication system based on individual postings and replies, which form so-called threads. Discussion forums usually focus on one topic, typically divided into individual sub-forums [Bächle, 2005]. They can be implemented as stand-alone Web sites, or, more often, be integrated into other Web-based applications or Web-based educational systems [Helic et al., 2004b].

Web-based discussion forums are based on the system of *Usenet* newsgroups, which has existed since 1979 [LaQuey, 1990]. Usenet is based on the general purpose Unix-to-Unix Copy Program (UUCP). In contrast to discussion forums, Usenet newsgroups require software separate from the browser, the so-called newsreaders, to be accessed. Another related application is a *mailing list*, which maps the newsgroup paradigm on individual e-mail messages sent to all of the registered participants of a mailing lit.

While *Usenet* is close enough to Web-based discussion forums as far as the type of communication is concerned, there are a number of differences aside from the technical implementation [Möller, 2006]:

⊕ The possibility of using numerous graphical smileys

⊕ The ease of embedding images into postings

⊕ Avatars as graphic representation of the authors

⊕ An active moderation team, which actually deletes and moves postings, or locks threads

⊕ Some kind of ranking system for active authors

Forums are usually administrated by *moderators* and *administrators*, which are, beside technical responsibilities in the case of administrators, mainly responsible for the surveillance of forum rules, so-called policies. Various policies exist concerning the anonymity of forum authors, respectively the need to register and post using a nickname or real name. Rules concerning the social interaction are summarized as *netiquette*.

Communication within discussion forums may be inhibited by trolls or *spammers*. Trolls are users who deliberately break the netiquette and post insulting messaged in order to bait other users into losing their temper. This often results in the so-called *flame-wars*, when the discussion turns personal and heated instead of focusing on a subject. Spammers are individual or autonomous programs, the so-called spam bots, which post messages for advertisement reasons and likewise add no information on a topic.

2.1.1.2 Microblogging

The term microblogging relates to weblogs (described below), but describes a far more communication-oriented technology. It can be defined as *"a small-scale form of blogging, generally made up of short, succinct messages, used by both consumers and businesses to share news, post status updates, and carry on conversation"* [Templeton,

2008]. The basic application is the publication of information about the users' own daily lives. It is used for the following types of user intentions [Java et al., 2007]:

- Daily chatter
- Conversations
- Sharing information
- Reporting news

The best-known example of microblogging services is the largest platform worldwide, Twitter[5] [Griswold, 2007]. Microblogging consists of posing individual, short messages, usually no longer than 140 characters, to the user's feed. In the case of twitter, these messages are called tweets. Either sending a direct message, or replying to other users' tweets by adding `@username` to one's own tweets conducts communication with other users. Tweets by other users are forwarded by using the tag `RT @username`, thus tributing the original author. This *re-tweeting* is one of the basic mechanisms to spread news in the microblogging context.

Usually microbloggers subscribe to other users' feeds and become *followers*, in order to retrieve an aggregated feed of all their fields of interest. The number of followers has evolved into a status symbol for the individual microbloggers which leads to a contest between US celebrity Ashton Kutcher and the news network CNN over the first microblog with more than 1 million followers[6], which resulted in the celebrity's account being the first twitter account with this number of followers in April 2009[7].

Microblogging is a form of informal communication, consisting of unplanned, and brief "catching-up", comparable to "water-cooler conversations". A number of benefits

---

[5] http://www.twitter.com/, accessed 2009-09-04

[6] http://www.cnn.com/2009/TECH/04/15/ashton.cnn.twitter.battle/index.html, accessed 2009-11-06

[7] http://www.techcrunch.com/2009/04/16/kutcher-plays-his-pied-piper-flute-and-gets-a-millions/, accessed 2009-11-06

deriving from such informal communication has been identified. First of all this communication provides a common ground for a community, extending mutual understanding. Secondly it creates a feeling of intimacy and connectedness. Moreover it improves the personal perception among the individuals of a community. Finally, it may lead to the acquisition of valuable information for the individuals. [Zhao and Rosson, 2009]

The application of the concept of microblogging in a collaborative authoring setting is discussed in chapter 8.7.

2.1.1.3 Social Networking

Social networking, although no new phenomenon, has gained tremendous importance and publicity in the recent years. Sites like xing.com[8] or facebook.com[9] are among the fastest growing services in the Web. With more than 67% of Internet users worldwide using social networking sites each month and spending 10% of their online time on this type of application, social networks have become the fourth most popular online category, ahead of personal e-mail. [Nielsen, 2009]

Social networking sites are defined as web-based services aimed to visualize and maintain the social network of the users. The key functionality consists of (a) the ability to create and maintain a public profile, usually including multi-layered options for privacy control of the individual types of personal information included, (b) the ability to articulate a list of connected users, and (c) the possibility to view and traverse along the lines of connections between the individual users. The individual social networking sites use varying nomenclatures for these concepts. [Boyd and Ellison, 2007]

---

[8] http://www.xing.com/ accessed 2009-11-12
[9] http://www.facebook.com/ accessed 2009-11-12

Most existing social networks are focused on a primary target group, like business contacts for xing.com, or students for studivz.net[10]. More generally, social networks focused on business and private contacts can be discerned. Communication is conducted among the connected users of a network as well as within *groups*, which resemble discussion forums for communities of interest. [Heidemann, 2009]

The structure of social networks can be mapped onto graphs consisting of nodes (users) and edges (relations) [Koch et al., 2007]. The topology of such graphs is the key to the scientific research on the networks (cf. 0). Nodes with numerous edges, so called *hubs*, are of special interest in this context.

Already in the 1960's Milgram proposed the *small world phenomenon*, stating that every person would be separated from every other person by averagely 6 connections [Milgram, 1967]. In the context of social networks this theory has been investigated by Microsoft Research, who discovered an average path length of 6.6 between two nodes in the graphs [Leskovec and Horvitz, 2008].

As far as the usefulness of such social networks is concerned, Metcalfe's Law concerning the usefulness of online communities can be applied. It states that the usefulness of such a community is proportional to the square number of other users [Shapiro and Varian, 1999].

Social networks face a number of challenges. One of them is the privacy of the personal information about the users and the privacy of the conversations between them. Current privacy features of the most popular social networks have been shown to be inadequate [Poller, 2008]. Other challenges include the missing or vague business concepts of the individual platforms and the sustainability of the added value which these platforms provide for their users.

---

[10] http://www.studivz.net accessed 2009-11-12

2.1.2 Collaboration

The second of the essential components of the superordinate concept of *social media* is *collaboration*. This term describes the act of working "jointly with others or together especially in an intellectual endeavor" [Merriam-Webster, 2009]. As far as information technology is concerned the corresponding field of research is usually referred to as computer supported collaborative work (CSCW), a term originating from a workshop on "the application of technologies for support on the workplace" by Greif and Cashman in 1984 [Kunow and Schwickert, 1999].

Table 2-1: Time / Space Model according to Johansen [Johansen, 1988].

	One meeting site (same places)	Multiple meeting sites (different places)
Synchronous communication (same time)	Face to Face Interactions	Remote Interactions
	✘ Public computer displays ✘ Electronic meeting rooms ✘ Group decision support systems	✘ Shared view desktop conferencing systems ✘ Desktop conferencing with collaborative editors ✘ Video conferencing ✘ Media spaces
Asynchronous communication (different time)	Ongoing Tasks	Communication and Coordination
	✘ Team rooms ✘ Group displays ✘ Shift work groupware ✘ Project management	✘ Vanilla email ✘ Asynchronous conferencing bulletin boards ✘ Structured messaging systems ✘ Workflow management ✘ Version control ✘ Meeting schedulers ✘ Cooperative hypertext & organizational memory

Software-assisted collaboration can provide asynchronous tools, like e-mail, as well as complex synchronous tools [Tochtermann and Schwartz, 2000]. A second possible categorization for collaboration tools is discrimination by space into tools supporting groups in the same location and tools supporting collaboration over distance. Table 2-1 presents a list of sample collaborative applications in the context of these two classifications.

However, communication applications can be seen as basic applications for collaborative work, more sophisticated applications have been developed meanwhile. The most prominent collaborative tool associated with the Social Web is presented in the next paragraphs.

2.1.2.1 Wikis

Wikis have become the archetypical online collaboration tool in the last 10 years. The term wiki was originally introduced by Leuf and Cunningham in 1995 [Leuf and Cunningham, 2001]. The *WikiWikiWeb* was the first collaborative online authoring tool, although the underlying concepts can be based to the origins of hypertext [Bush, 1945].

The term *wiki* itself derives from the Hawaiian term *wikiwiki*, meaning "very quick". Cunningham had learned the term when traveling with the "wiki wiki bus", a shuttle bus from Honolulu Airport, and decided to use this term instead of calling his new technology "quick web", to avoid undesired connotations. [Cunningham, 2005]

A wiki is a tool enabling web pages to be collaboratively edited online. It is based on a simplified markup language used to create the pages within the browser. Hyperlinks can point to other wiki pages or external Web pages. This classification allows the creation of backlinks, listing all pages that link to the current page, as well as the prevention of broken links due to deletion or renaming.

The core collaboration support of this technology is the detailed tracing of changes in a document to the corresponding author. All changes are available with time, date, and user information in a document history. Each individual change can be reverted.

Based on the original concept of WikiWikiWeb, numerous other wikis have been developed. Among the most popular wikis are the file based TWiki[11] which is ideal for small wiki instances, and Mediawiki[12].

Mediawiki is the underlying technology for the probably best-known wiki: Wikipedia. Wikipedia is a user-created and user-maintained online encyclopedia. It had outnumbered offline encyclopedias, as far as the number of articles is concerned, by 2005 with more than 1.5 million articles [Voss, 2005]. Wikipedia is based on collaborative authoring of the encyclopedic content by registered and unregistered users alike, and on free licensing of images and texts. The corresponding licenses do not only include the freedom of charge, but also the freedom to modify and reuse the material, albeit only under another free license. Wikipedia is operated by the Wikimedia foundation[13], a non-profit charitable organization.

Wikipedia has been facing criticism concerning the quality of the articles and the traceability of the individual content to the contributors over the years. There are three main concerns in this context. Firstly, pages are created by multiple, possibly even anonymous authors. Secondly, pages can constantly be modified. Thirdly, the presented information may be biased.

In order to solve these issues the Wikimedia foundation has equally been working on solutions for the problems identified. For example, although the individual articles in Wikipedia can constantly be modified, access to former version remains available via *permalinks*. The creation of new articles or deletion of articles is no longer available for

---

[11] http://twiki.org/ accessed 2009-11-19

[12] http://www.mediawiki.org/wiki/MediaWiki/de accessed 2009-11-19

[13] http://wikimediafoundation.org/ accessed 2010-03-18

unregistered users. *Sighted versions* have been introduced to confirm the validity of content by experts. Moreover, markings for excellent articles have been introduced. Chapter 2.3.1 deals with Wikipedia and possible criticism in detail.

2.1.3 Sharing

In the context of this book, the term sharing is used for those aspects of social media, which are focused on the publication of content, and the provision of resources and information to a community of interest. In a broader sense, this also encompasses the sharing of data as in file sharing networks.

2.1.3.1 Social Bookmarking

Social bookmarking is a collaborative concept based on the notion of sharing bookmarks and thus enhancing the effectiveness for searching contents in the Web. For the collaborating users social bookmarking tools provide powerful meanings to organize their own bookmarks, yet the core benefit lies in the integration of the references and added information from many users, as manually created reference collections provide trustful information sources due to the usually high quality [Yanbe et al., 2007].

The collaborating users can publish their bookmarks on a social bookmarking site and add metadata as description. This metadata is usually added as tags. A *tag* is an arbitrary, non-hierarchical keyword. Usually, three to five tags per tagged item provide the best results for the quality of ensuing search results. In the case of social bookmarking these tags allow the organization and display the individual user's collection with meaningful labels [Millen et al., 2005].

In order to provide a navigational tool for tags, *tag clouds* have emerged as an alternative to traditional forms of navigation. A *tag cloud* is a list of the applied tags, usually displayed alphabetically sorted in one large paragraph. In this tag cloud, the frequency of the use of individual tag clouds is usually indicated by the font size of this individual tag. This provides the user with both, the alphabetical and the frequency information, in a single navigational structure [Millen et al., 2006].

Social bookmarking sites like del.icio.us[14] integrate the manually created reference collections of their users to provide interesting bookmarks by novelty or popularity. Moreover searching for tags or the exploration of tag clouds are provided. Bibsonomy[15] provides a comparable approach for scientific references, integrating bookmarks with references to publications.

2.1.3.2 Blogs

A weblog, usually also referred to as with the contracted term *blog*, is a "log of the web", a term coined by Barger in 1997 [Paquet, 2003]. The entries in such a weblog, the so-called posts are presented in reverse chronological order. This type of websites is used for various applications, from the publication of news on a particular topic, to personal online diaries. Blogs may be maintained either by individuals, or by a community of authors. Due to the possibilities of weblogs, they are also applied to *grassroots journalism*, where bloggers instead of journalists are a source for news.

The social aspect of blogs arises from the interconnections in the communities of bloggers. Weblog software usually provides the possibility for comments and trackbacks. These are applied to connect blogs as well as bloggers.

Usually weblog software provides the possibility for readers to comment every single post, either anonymously, or by providing the user's name and a link to the own website or blog. Systems like Gravatar[16] provide means for the commentators to identify themselves with their unique only identity, a so-called *avatar*.

A *trackback* is a technology, which allows weblogs to be automatically notified when other weblogs link to individual posts and create backward links [Six Apart, 2004].

---

[14] http://del.icio.us, accessed 2010-02-17
[15] http://bibsonomy.org, accessed 2010-02-17
[16] http://www.gravatar.com, accessed 2010-02-17

These backward links, including the linking site's name, the post title and an excerpt, are added at the bottom of the referenced blog post.

Trackbacks, comments and link lists to befriended bloggers, so called blogrolls, provide a network of links between individual weblogs. In such a way, a distributed, collective and interlinked blogosphere is created. Over 70% of the communities in this blogosphere are can be relayed to three factors in common: age, location, and interest. These communities shown bursts of activity, which can be tracked over time. [Kumar et al., 2004]

Based on the links between blogs in the blogosphere and a categorization of topics, the standing and influence of individual blogs in the blogosphere can be calculated. The foremost site calculating such blog rankings is Technorati[17].

Although weblogs are used for a number of motivations, they are also applied to support group collaboration and community [Nardi et al., 2004]. They can be applied to loose communities of interest, as well as in communities of practice or workgroups.

Chapter 2.2 deals with the success factors in a blogging community more closely. Furthermore, Chapter 5 takes a closer look at the possible application of weblogs for self-reflection in technology-enhanced learning.

2.1.3.3 Podcasting

Podcasting is the audio equivalent of the easy publishing provided by weblogs. It is the creation and distribution of audio files via the Internet. This distribution is achieved by providing means of subscribing to the podcast and have the listeners automatically receive new publications. [Richardson, 2006]

The term *podcast*, according to Merriam-Webster's Online Dictionary[18], is an etymology derived from the archetypical trademark for a portable media player, *iPod*,

---

[17] http://technorati.com, accessed 2010-02-17

[18] http://www.merriam-webster.com/dictionary/podcast, accesses 2010-02-17

and the term broad*cast*. Despite the reference to Apple's media player, podcasts can technically be used with any portable or non-portable media player.

The subscription of a podcast is achieved by subscribing to an RSS feed. The abbreviation stands for "Rich Site Summary" or "Real Simple Syndication". This XML file format provides means for device-independent publication of the content and the syndication of updates by the clients. The RSS information available on such a site is called RSS feed [Duffy and Bruns, 2006].

In the case of podcasts the client software used to subscribe to the RSS feed automatically downloads the news content on the computer. When connecting a mobile media player to the client, the content is also synchronized with this device.

As the term *podcast* is restricted to audio files, supplementary terms have been created for other types of content. A *vodcast* is commonly understood as a video podcast. Another example is a *screencast*, which describes the publication of screen-captured videos and tutorials.

As far as the publication of content is concerned, podcasts cannot qualify as social media for the lack of communication involved. However, they qualify as social media as soon as more than the explicit audio broadcast is concerned. With the possibility to comment on podcasts, refer to other podcasts in a dialog, podcasting sites provide some key features which identify social media [Jensen, 2008].

2.1.3.4 Multimedia Sharing

Numerous other Social Web sites have been created to provide the possibility to share multimedia content. These sites have key social media features in common like the ease of publication, the possibility to comment and rate the published content, as well as to link and refer to other users' content.

YouTube[19] has evolved into the archetypical video-sharing portal. The site is focused on the publication of user-created content as well as professionally-created content, which indeed encompasses a great part of the published videos [Kruitbosch and Nack, 2008].

As far as image sharing is concerned, Picasa[20] and Flickr[21] can be considered as the most important examples for this type of service. Both focus on the free upload of images to share with friends and family, or to make them available for the public. Images can be tagged, geo-located and organized.

Finally, other types of more specialized sharing sites exist. Slideshare[22], i.e., is focused on the publication of PowerPoint slides. Another specialized example is Codepad[23], which can be used to share program code by software developers.

After this general introduction into the core concepts and features of social media applications, a closer look on two Social Web applications will be presented. As far as students are concerned, weblogs and wikis have been shown to be the most widely used applications [Safran et al., 2007a].

2.2 Success Factors in a Weblog Community

User generated content published via weblogs has gained importance in the last years, and the number of globally available weblogs increases. However, a large fraction of these shows low publishing activity and are rarely read. This section is a quantitative analysis of success factors in a community of over 15.000 weblogs, hosted by a local Austrian newspaper. We looked at publishing activity by content type, community

---

[19] http://youtube.com, accessed 2010-02-17
[20] http://picasa.google.com/, accessed 2010-02-18
[21] http://flickr.com/, accessed 2010-02-18
[22] http://www.slideshare.net/, accessed 2010-02-18
[23] http://codepad.org/, accessed 2010-02-18

activity and writing style. In addition, the interconnectedness of the community was analyzed.

2.2.1 Introduction

In the age of the so-called Web 2.0, user generated content is credited increasing importance, as *participation* is one of the key characteristics of this concept [O'Reilly, 2005] . In the context of journalism the generation of news content by users, also called *citizen journalism* or *grassroots journalism* [Gillmor, 2004], is gradually complementing and, in some cases, even contesting information provided in a classic, publishing environment. Especially in the news domain, weblogs have become an important source of information beside newspaper websites. This section will focus on such *user-generated content* published via weblogs hosted by an Austrian newspaper.

The key question in this context is: What makes a weblog successful? In the context of this research, the number of visits to a weblog is used to measure success. For the use in this analysis, visits were counted as unique IP addresses, counting a new visit after 20 minutes of inactivity. So, the question can be reformulated as: what are the factors that lead to a high number of visits of the content created by the users?

Another interesting aspect of user-generated content is the community of the involved users. Questions in this context concern the structure of this community. Is the community divided into smaller communities or is there a central group of active users?

2.2.2 Related Work

Quite a lot of research on weblogs has been published in the recent years. Interesting in this context are publications on ranking weblogs like [Kritikopoulos et al., 2006]. The authors presented a modification of the PageRank algorithm [Page et al., 1999] designed to take into account the links between the weblogs and the similarity of the users, as well as links to non-weblog URLs. The target is to rank weblogs by importance.

[Du and Wagner, 2006] tried to answer the question for success factors of weblogs from a technology perspective. The study analyzed the impact of technology used on the success of 126 blogs taken from the top 100 listings of the Technorati[24] website. In the case of Technorati, the number of inbound links to a weblog measures success.

As far as the analysis of weblogs communities is concerned, [Cohen and Krishnamurthy, 2006] count connections by hyperlinks and relation by type or topic as possible relations forming communities of weblogs. This point of view focuses on the relations provided in the content of the weblog. A complementing approach, as presented in [Li et al., 2007] takes the information available from the guest comments to the entries into account.

Figure 2-1: *Meine Kleine* weblogs

---

[24] http://www.technorati.com, accessed 2009-04-22

2.2.3 The Analysis

The "*Meine Kleine*" weblogs[25] of the local Austrian "*Kleine Zeitung*" newspaper offer a promising possibility to take a closer look at a large number of weblogs in a relatively closed environment. Users of this environment have the ability to publish text and images (photos) to their own weblogs. In addition, comments as guestbook entries can be written to the weblogs of other users. Figure 2-1 displays the main page of *Meine Kleine* blogspace.

By November 21 2006, the blogspace consisted of 15702 active blogs, ranging from topical weblogs by the newspaper's editors to private diaries of individual readers. In our research, we had access to the servers log files as well as the database holding the weblog entries. The log files and entries from October 7 to November 21 2006 (about 6 weeks) were analyzed in the course of this project.

2.2.3.1 Basic Statistics

The community of *Kleine Zeitung* readers consisted of a large number of more than 118,000 registered users. Of those users, 15702 have activated the weblog for their account and had at least one visit in the analyzed 6-week period. 560 of those bloggers were active publishers in this period, meaning that they added content to their weblog in these 6 weeks. This, together with the fact that only the top 1730 weblogs had five or more visits in this period, resulted in our decision to take only the 2000 most visited weblogs into account for all further examinations (see Figure 2-2).

The publishing activity of the examined users was quite incoherent. The number of (text) entries published ranged from 0 to 45 for the individual blogs. The most active poster of images published 469 images in the examined period. As far as the activity in the community is concerned, the most active users posted 80 comments and 137 guestbook entries in other users' weblogs. Figure 2-3 shows the summary of publishing activity for the users with the 20 most-visited weblogs.

---

[25] http://www.meinekleine.at, accessed 2009-04-22

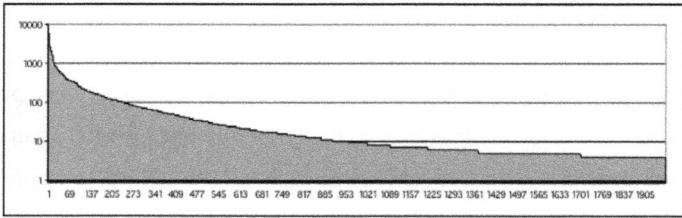

Figure 2-2: Number of visits of the top 2000 weblogs

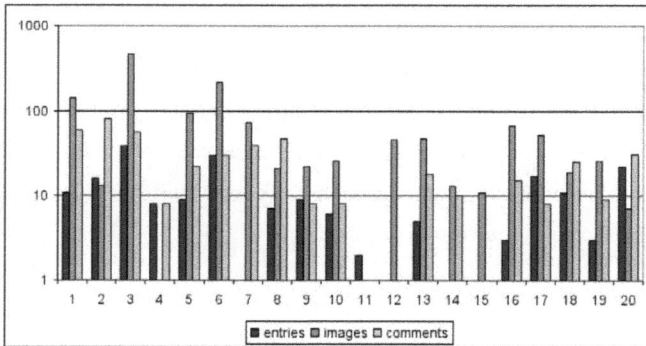

Figure 2-3: Publishing activity of the 20 most-visited users

2.2.3.2 Activity of Authors vs. Readers by Time of Day

Beside the basic statistics of the weblogs, an investigation of the user activity in the course of a day has been carried out. This focused on the access of readers to the weblogs as well as on authoring activity by the users.

On the one hand, the activity of the content authors, those users creating text entries or uploading photos, shows an almost even distribution throughout the day, with one peak at noon and one in the early evening. This is in contrast to our assumption that most users would be contributing content to their blogs in the evening and in a home environment. This assumption is true, however, for the posting of comments, which mainly occurs between 19:00 and 22:00.

Figure 2-4 shows the significantly different graphs for publishing own content versus activity in the community (i.e. writing comments and guestbook entries in other users' weblogs).

On the other hand, the activity of the visitors of the blogs in the course of a day was also investigated and viewed separately for the different types of content. As with the authoring activity, reading is almost evenly distributed from 7:00 to 23:00. Peak usage is from 19:00 to 22:00, which corresponds to the peak in commenting. The visits of guestbook entries vary from this general observation, as they have a peak in the early afternoon and none in the evening (see Figure 2-5).

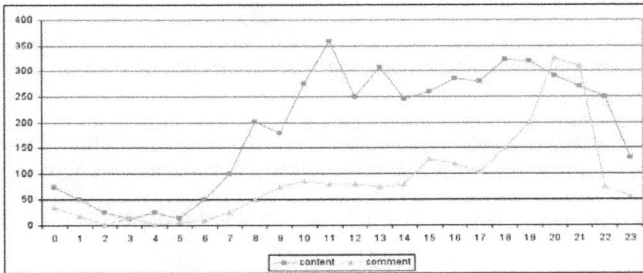

Figure 2-4: Content and comments in the course of the day

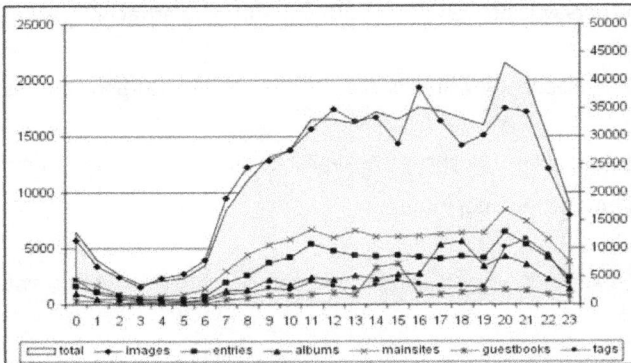

Figure 2-5: Access to content types in the course of the day

2.2.3.3 Influences on Popularity

The focus of the research on the *Meine Kleine* blogspace was to find and verify factors for the success of weblogs. We decided to analyze nine possible criteria, arranged into three groups. These criteria were chosen based on the available data from the server logs and after intense discussion with those editors responsible for the blogspace of "Kleine Zeitung Digital" concerning their experience and assumptions. Together with these editors, nine hypotheses were formulated. These hypotheses were tested by calculating the Pearson's correlation coefficients for the variables concerned and verifying the significance with a Student's t-test at a confidence level of 0.99

Table 2-2: hypotheses for weblog popularity

H_1	Authors who write more posts attract more visitors.
H_2	Authors who provide more images attract more visitors.
H_3	Authors who provide new content more often attract more visitors.
H_4	Authors who actively comment other weblogs attract more visitors.
H_5	More frequently visited authors receive more comments.
H_6	Authors who actively post in other guestbooks attract more visitors.
H_7	More frequently visited authors receive more guestbook entries.
H_8	Authors whose postings are similar to the writing style of newspaper editors attract more visitors.
H_9	The posts of frequently visited authors are similar in writing style.

2.2.3.4 Influence of Content Types provided

In a first step, the different types of content composing the weblog were analyzed on their impact on the popularity. The visits of the individual blogs were compared to the number of textual entries (H_1), images (H_2) and the days the user was active (H_3) in the period investigated. *Textual entries* are all posts in the weblog, regardless of the fact whether images were also included or not. *Images* are all image files and photos in the weblog. This results in the fact that an entry with photos is counted as textual entry as well as image. Figure 2-6 depicts the activity for the 20 top-scoring weblogs in these categories.

The value of *active days* gives an overview of the activity of the author within the six-week period of data collection. It encompasses all days the user has actively contributed to his weblog.

The highest correlation of content type to popularity could be found with the user's active days (H_3), being 0.68. The correlation to the entries (H_1) and images (H_2) were lower, at 0.60 and 0.53, respectively.

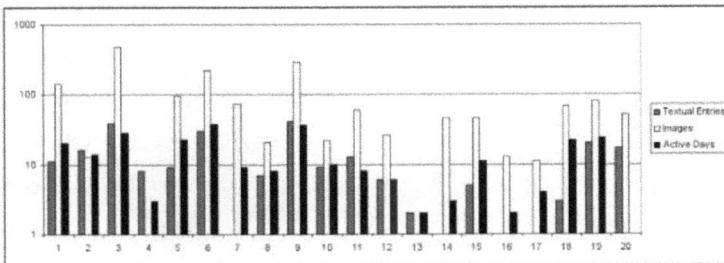

Figure 2-6: Content provided by the 20 most-visited bloggers

2.2.3.5 Influence of Community Activity

Secondly, the influence of community activity was investigated. We decided to analyze the correlation of comment and guestbook activity, outbound as well as inbound. Trackbacks were not considered because this technology is not available for "Meine

Kleine" weblogs. Figure 2-7 depicts the activity for the 20 top-scoring weblogs in these categories.

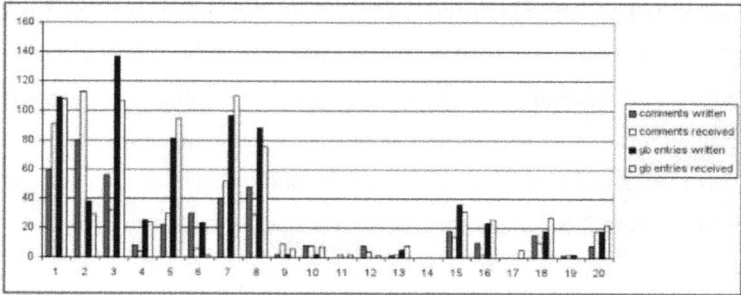

Figure 2-7: Activity of the 20 most-visited bloggers

The highest value was found for the obvious correlation of received comments and visits to the weblog with 0.77 (H5). The number of guestbook entries received correlates with 0.69 (H7). For own comments (H4) and guestbook entries in other blogs (H6), the correlations are 0.70 and 0.68, respectively (see Table 2-3).

It should be noted that these correlations coefficients are higher than those of publishing content are. In other words, in order to have a highly visible weblog, it is even more important to be active in the community than to publish own content regularly! This is true for the individual correlations as well as for the summary of content provided respectively own community activity. There is a total correlation of 0.61 of content provided to the number of visits, while the correlation of community-activity to number of visits is 0.71.

2.2.4 Influence of Writing Style

A further aspect of the research investigated upon the contents of the *Kleine Zeitung* blogspace is the influence of the author's writing style. For this purpose, the similarity computation of the Autonomy Search Engine which is based on Bayesian inference [Autonomy Inc., 2007], was used. Bayesian inference is a method of statistics which is based on the analysis of evidence, which is consistent or inconsistent with a given hypotheses. In contrast to sampling theory, which is based on an hypotheses and a null hypothesis, and the rejection of one of these, the Bayesian approach tries to make inferences that take into account all available information [MacKay, 2003].

In a first step, the similarity of top-scoring blogs to news articles was compared, in an attempt to verify the influence of *grassroots journalism* on popularity. Individual weblog entries of the top 2000 blogs were compared to the editorial blogs of the Kleine Zeitung (written by professional journalists) and to the top five blogs. This first approach led to no significant results.

In a next step, the coherence of the contents of the top scoring blogs was analyzed. We compared the similarity of a summary document containing all weblog entries of one user with the top scoring editorial weblog and the top scoring user weblog. With these conditions, we found a correlation of 0.38 for the similarity to the editorial weblog (H_8) and a correlation of 0.25 for the similarity to the top scoring user weblog (H_9). Both correlations are lower than those for the content type and user activity. Figure 2-8 shows the similarity to the top scoring editorial weblog and the top scoring user weblog for the 20 most visited weblogs.

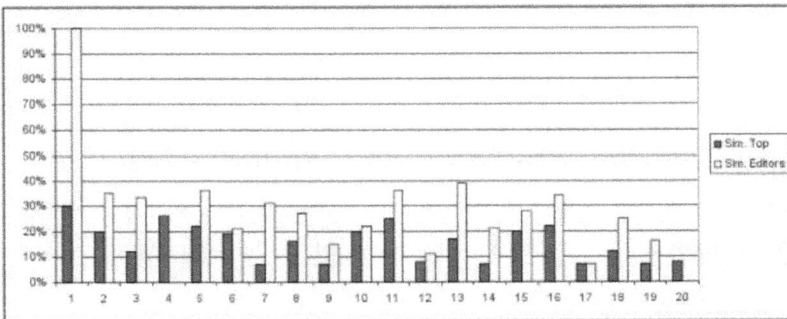

Figure 2-8: Similarity of the 20 most-visited blogs with editorial content and the top-ranked blog

Table 2-3: Summary of correlations

Number of visits correlated to	Hypotheses	Correlation	T-test	Conf. interval
Active days	H_1	0.68	41.46	0.99
# of posts written	H_2	0.60	33.52	0.99
# of images uploaded	H_3	0.53	27.94	0.99
# of comments given	H_4	0.70	43.81	0.99
# of comments received	H_5	0.77	53.94	0.99
# of guestbook entries given	H_6	0.68	41.46	0.99
# of guestbook entries received	H_7	0.69	42.61	0.99
Similarity to top rated user	H_8	0.25	11.54	0.99
Similarity to editorial blogs	H_9	0.38	18.36	0.99

2.2.4.1 Conclusions

All of the investigated success factors have a positive correlation with the number of visits, in each case statistically significant with a degree of freedom of 1998 (2000 samples) and a confidence interval of 0.99. This means all nine hypotheses can be confirmed. The highest correlations can be found for the activity in the blogging community. Table 2-3 illustrates the correlations of the individual factors.

2.2.5 Communities in "Meine Kleine" weblogs

As shown in the previous chapter, the activity within the community is a crucial factor for the success of a weblog. In a final step of our research, we tried to visualize the communication between the community members by comments and guestbook entries. We used the *prefuse*[26] framework to visualize a GraphML representation [Brandes et al., 2002] of users and their connections. GraphML is an XML file format for graphs. Structural elements in GraphML are added as <edge> and <node> elements, with the possibility to color the nodes and assign weights to the edges.

In the resulting graphs, the members of the community are depicted as nodes and links resulting from comments or guestbook entries as edges. A Fruchterman-Reingold force-directed placement algorithm [Fruchtermann and Reingold, 1991] was chosen for the graph for a comprehensive visualization of the interconnectedness of the community. An initial version of the community graph containing all communications turned out to be too complex.

In order to produce clearly arranged graphs, the number of community members taken into account was reduced. As the twenty users with the highest numbers of visits were responsible for 91% of the community activity, only these twenty and the corresponding conversational partners were taken into account.

In the resulting Figure 2-9 nodes representing the 20 most-visited weblogs are presented in darker shade than the others are. Four of these top-twenty users have did not give any comments or create guestbook entries in the analyzed period and were thus removed from the graph. The remaining 16 top-scorers form a tight network with several communities unique to individual users, and thus can be classified as hubs.

To further clarify the social network of the Kleine Zeitung blogspace, only those edges were taken into account that represented three or more communication activities. The resulting graph shows a tight network of eleven of the top score users, while the remaining nine have no connections to the graph (Figure 2-10). Four of these eleven users also build their own sub graphs of community activities.

---

[26] http://prefuse.org/, accessed 2009-04-22

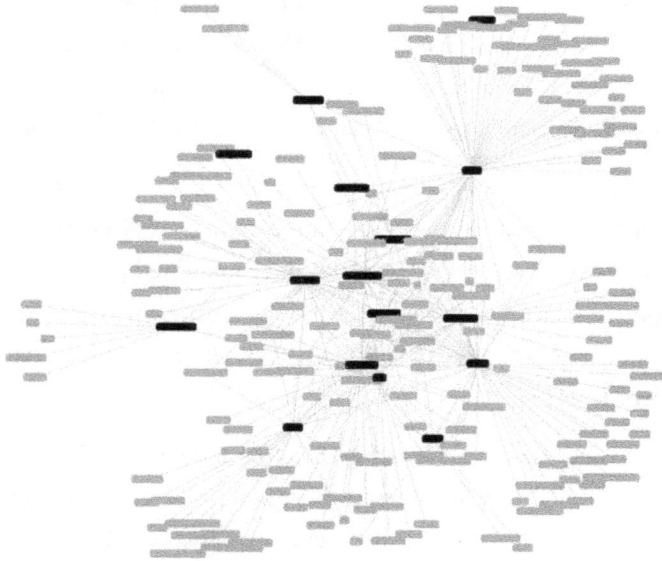

Figure 2-9: Force-directed placement of the 20 most-visited users and their contacts[27]

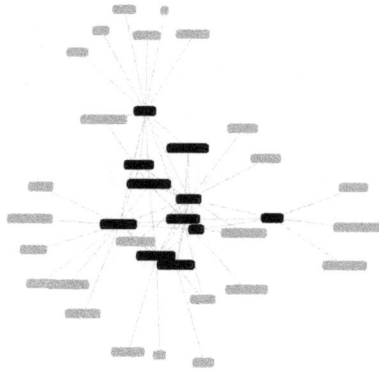

Figure 2-10: The community of the most-visited users

---

[27] For privacy reasons the user names have been blackened in the community graphs.

2.2.6 Conclusions

The analysis on the blogspace of the *Kleine Zeitung* online community was conducted to find key factors for success of weblogs. The factors activity, number of textual entries, number of images, comments given, comments received, guestbook entries given and guestbook entries received were analyzed in this context. The comparison of the influence of these nine factors showed that the most important of these factors are the community activities of the authors, i.e. writing comments and guestbook entries in other blogs.

2.3 Collaborative Systems - Beyond Wikipedia

Although Wikipedia is doubtlessly considered to be the leading collaborative system for knowledge acquisition, there is still need for alternative scenarios to satisfy more specialized scenarios than a general knowledge need.

2.3.1 Several Problems with Wikipedia

There is a substantial list of potential problems, with a few of them having been addressed (particularly in the English version) to some extent recently. A brief look is provided at some of the problems in what follows.

2.3.1.1 Contributions can be erroneous.

Taking into account that the contributions are written by a wide range of persons this is not surprising. First, sometimes there is no objective or unique truth. Take as a good example the history of the first lunar landing. Now there are almost as many people, who believe that Neil Armstrong did not step on the moon, as there are persons believing he did. Since videos etc. can be faked, nobody except some of the persons directly involved can really be sure of what the truth is. Second, some errors may occur just through typos or other kinds of sloppiness. Thirdly, some errors may be introduced on purpose to let something or somebody look better or worse than is the case in reality. Fourthly, stories may be introduced just as jokes. A good example is the list of the most famous computer scientists of Austria that was available for weeks on the German Wikipedia, and listed in spot number two a young student: it was exactly that student who posted the story as a joke. The fact that Wikipedia contains mistakes is not troublesome by itself. After all, even the most prestigious well-edited encyclopedia will not be completely error-free. However, that an increasing number of people consider what they read in Wikipedia as objective truth, despite the fact that it should be taken with more than a grain of salt!

2.3.1.2 Contributions can be incomplete.

Incompleteness is often more disturbing than just encountering mistakes. The statement that "Scientist x has 12 publications" may not be wrong, but if that particular scientist has indeed 200 publications it is certainly grossly misleading. "Among the big cities in New Zealand are Auckland, Wellington and Dunedin" is certainly not wrong, but it leaves the impression that those are the most important ones, downgrading the role of e.g. Christchurch, a city considerably bigger than Dunedin, and omitting a number of cities comparable in importance to Dunedin, like Hamilton, Nelson or Gisborne.

2.3.1.3 Contributions can be slanderous.

Certainly, the first and hence most famous incident was the "Seigenthaler case. An anonymous person wrote a defamatory contribution in the Wikipedia that remained undetected for almost four months. When the contribution was pointed out to Seigenthaler, he demanded that the writer be found out or else he would sue Wikipedia. The writer was indeed found out and eventually the row subdued. However, it is typical that even today's contribution on the controversy in the Wikipedia is actually omitting the uproar this case caused, another example that omissions are often more misleading than errors!

2.3.1.4 Material on a person is outside the control of the person involved.

The Seigenthaler case mentioned is one example of this. However, even if no slander is involved, the control on information about oneself in Wikipedia is limited. A famous story is the "Brandt case": a contribution written about Daniel Brandt was not to Brandt's liking; when he changed it, an anonymous user switched it back to the old version. In addition, this process continued a number of times to the frustration of Brandt.

Finally, Brandt was barred from further editing. Brandt has been and continues to be a staunch critic of Wikipedia. For instance, Brandt's view is "that the creation of biographical articles on Wikipedia is broadly unacceptable due to the inaccuracy of information included and a lack of accountability". Just in passing, let us mention that Daniel Brandt was the one who found out the person behind the defamatory information on Seigenthaler.

2.3.1.5 Contributions can be unstable.

The most famous case is certainly the comments on Kerry and Bush in the 2004 election for president of the US: both stories were completely exchanged by editors of the opposing more than 10.000 times.

2.3.1.6 Material can be strongly biased.

There are numerous examples of this. Typically, a "fan club" will extol the virtues of a person, a location, a product, etc. One instance that is by far not the most blatant case, yet is often mentioned, is the variety of contributions on Paul Morphy, a famous chess player born in the US in 1837. In the English version, some 10 pages are dedicated to him, in the German only 4 and in the French just ½ page, although German and French Wikipedia are very similar in size.

2.3.1.7 Material can be contradictory.

There are a number of cases where e.g. the description of a country gives a figure for the population of the capital city, but the contribution concerning the capital city sometimes gives a very different figure. Although this phenomenon is understandable (contributions are written by different people at different times using different sources), it shows that the "unifying hand", which usual encyclopedias are exposed to, is missing.

Looking at this list it might appear that Wikipedia is quite useless. However, nothing could be further from the truth. Despite the shortcomings, mentioned Wikipedia is a very useful source of information as long as one takes the contributions in it with a bit of caution.

Indeed, the quality of information is much better than one might expect. A number of tests have shown that the error- rate in Wikipedia is only some 25- 40% higher than in the best encyclopedias. The error rate is usually determined as follows. A sample of a few hundred random contributions is picked from a recognized Encyclopedia (like Britannica in English or Brockhaus in German). For each contribution, the corresponding one in Wikipedia is retrieved. When discrepancies are found, a further search is conducted, determining whether Wikipedia or the "classic" encyclopedia is correct.

2.3.2 The Alexander Project

In a research project at the *Institute for Information Systems and Computer Media* (IICM) of the *Graz University of Technology,* several aspects of adaptation in electronic encyclopedias were tested with a closed user. The *Alexander* project was based on the notion of combining a vast body of encyclopedic knowledge with contemporary news articles and fostering a community of interest engaged in the enrichment and expansion of this knowledge base.

As a source for encyclopedic entries *Alexander* was intended to draw upon a prime German encyclopedia - the digital *Brockhaus* encyclopedia [Bibliographisches Institut, 2009]. These entries should be complemented by articles from a large Austrian newspaper. Current articles should periodically be added to Alexander's database and kept for later reference. The members of the *Alexander* community should have the possibility to write their own articles and add them to the contents of the system.

2.3.2.1 Overview of Alexander's Functionality

Information retrieval in the knowledge base of encyclopedic and news contents was one of the core functionalities of *Alexander*. On the one hand, users could use a standard search approach to find articles on a topic of interest. Optionally all of the contents, the encyclopedic entries, the news articles or the community entries can be searched. On the other hand, users could pose questions to the system. These questions either could be general ones or be based on a certain article.

Two automatic approaches for answering the questions were used. In a first step, similar questions could be searched and presented to the user. In a second step, the natural language search facility of the *Brockhaus* encyclopedia could be used to find suiting articles in the content of the system.

As a second main aspect, *Alexander* offered the possibility for the user community to participate in the expansion of the content. Questions that could be answered automatically were relayed to the community for answering. Moreover, discussions, based on individual articles, were encouraged.

Users of *Alexander* were moreover encouraged to write own articles and add them to the Alexander knowledge base. Articles could be created "from scratch" or in relation to an existing article in the knowledge base. User-created articles were by default only editable by the author, but the latter had the possibility to set his work "community editable".

The Alexander community was a hierarchy of users based on the ideas presented in [Kolbitsch and Maurer, 2005]. The majority of users were classified as plain users, which could create content, have discussions and ask questions. Moreover, plain user had the possibility to rate the content created by other users or notify the higher-level users of potentially inappropriate content by marking it.

The quality of the community-generated content was verified by experts. As the prototype version of *Alexander* had a smaller user group than a live system, experts were not classified as domain experts and certified experts. The role of domain experts was held by a homogenous group of "expert users", which were entitled to answer questions and create content, like plain users. The content created by expert users was labeled in order to point out the potentially higher quality. Experts were moreover entitled to verify the appropriateness of marked content.

The higher hierarchical level of certified experts was presented by a "core expert group", which was responsible for the administration of the content. The users of the core expert group were entitled to modify and delete content created by other users. Moreover, the core expert group was responsible to find suitable experts in order to answer open questions.

2.3.2.2 Adaptability of the Alexander System

The prototype version of Alexander applied structural adaptation in several ways. In a first step, as *Alexander* was an application based on the Hyperwave Information Server [Hyperwave, 2009], made use of Hyperwave's link management. One of the advantages of this approach is the adaptation of links to documents, which were moved within the Alexander structure. Moreover, broken links were automatically removed.

In a second step, the main page of Alexander adapted to the user role and the current content of the knowledge base. While plain users only got the possibility to view the user-generated articles, the same link lead to a listing of all user-generated contents for expert users. Moreover, the main page contained the latest questions and recently modified or created articles. Figure 2-11 depicts the main page of the prototype implementation.

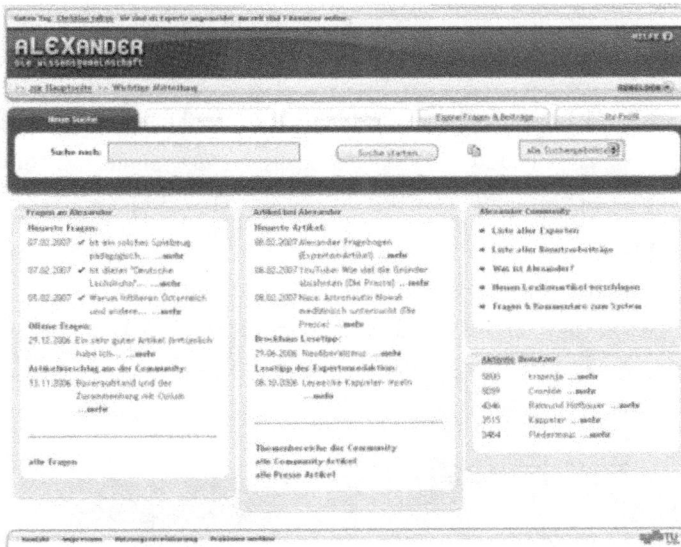

Figure 2-11: Screenshot of the Alexander prototype - main page

In a final step, the individual articles offered an adaptive list of related articles. The first part of this list consisted of user added external links and user generated articles which were written in relation to the current article. In a second part the full text search engine of *Hyperwave, Autonomy* [Autonomy Inc., 2007], was used to find related articles in the knowledge base. The type of articles presented depended on the current article. For encyclopedic articles, the related list consisted of news articles and vice versa. For user-generated articles this list consisted of encyclopedic, news and user generated articles.

2.3.2.3 Prototype Implementation

The *Alexander* project was evaluated at the Institute for *Information Systems and Computer Media* (IICM) at Graz University of Technology. Several aspects of collaboration and adaptation in electronic encyclopedias were tested with a closed user group of more than 700 individuals. *Alexander* was based on the notion of combining a vast body of encyclopedic knowledge with contemporary news articles and building an electronic community to develop and maintain this knowledge base [Presse, 2006].

As a source for encyclopedic entries, Alexander built on the *"Brockhaus Multimedial"*, with more than 185,000 textual entries and about 23,000 images [Bibliographisches Institut, 2005]. These articles were complemented with news stories from the online version of the *"Die Presse"*, a major Austrian newspaper [Presse, 2009]. As previously described the core functionality also consisted of current news being periodically added to Alexander's database and kept for reference. In addition to this, the members of the community could write new articles and add them to the knowledge base.

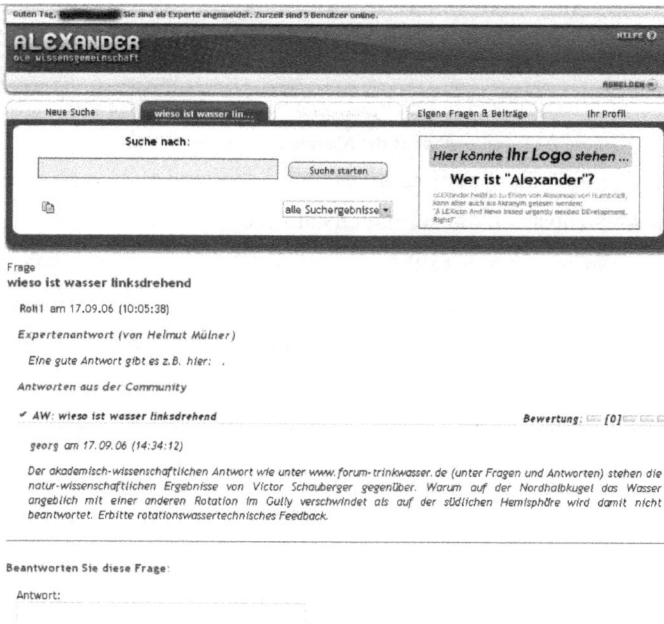

Figure 2-12: Screenshot of the Alexander prototype depicting a user question

A prototype evaluation of the system's core functionality was started in September 2006 and was scheduled to last at least three months. The test phase was designed to collect data on the acceptance of *Alexander's* key features and to gain experience in encyclopedias with both collaborative and adaptive features. The initial version of the prototype offered only the basic features concerning the encyclopedic, newspaper, and user articles, with new features gradually added to Alexander during the prototype period from September 6th, 2006 to January 31st, 2007The final version of the prototype additionally offered the features to post and answer questions, support expert and standard users, and dynamically includes image material of the German Press Agency (dpa[28]) for content. Several community features were included. Most prominently, users could rate any content of the system and collect the *activity score* for their actions in the system. As far as adaptive hypermedia is concerned, the prototype presented an up-to-date list of open questions, requested articles, newest newspaper articles, and reading tips. Moreover suiting newspaper and encyclopedic content was related to all entries and presented to the user. Figure 2-12 depicts a screenshot of a user question in the *Alexander* prototype.

The community of the prototype project and its activity was subsequently analyzed and compared to a more focused community of the German speaking *Platform Knowledge Management*[29]. The results were presented by [Dösinger et al., 2007]:

- 50% of the users spend the majority of their time (80-100%) reading

- 15% of the users accomplished between 50 and 500 interactions with the system, while the remaining 85% accomplished less than 50 interactions

- 61% of the users accessed the platform 1-2 times a week, while only 39% accesses it 1-2 times a month or less

- 51% of the users satisfied a concrete information need preferably with community content, 32% looked up lexical articles first, and 17% preferred the search in newspaper articles

---

[28] http://www.dpa.de, accessed 2009-04-20
[29] http://www.pwm.at/, accessed 2009-03-04

⊕ 55% of the users stated an information need for learning issues, 44% stated professional interest. 27% of the users used Alexander (also) to answer spare time related questions

⊕ The users of the prototype project showed a higher motivation for satisfying information needs than for disseminating and exchanging knowledge

⊕ As far as trust in community articles is concerned the majority of users trusted authors with a high qualification or a good evaluation most. Although Wikipedia is doubtlessly ranked the leading collaborative system for knowledge acquisition, there is still need for alternative scenarios to satisfy more specialized scenarios than a general knowledge need.

Especially in combination to the findings of the simultaneously evaluated *Platform Knowledge Management,* these results showed that the driving force for users in knowledge-based communities is the satisfaction of an information need. When evaluating information found in such communities, the qualification of the author seems to be the major influence. The common finding that passive consumers outnumber active contributors was approved. Finally, the findings of the evaluation showed that goals and purposes, as well as rules of behavior, should be introduced and clarified at the very beginning of a community project.

The experience taken from the Alexander project was used in the design of the ongoing follow-up project *Austria-Forum*[30], an online knowledge community focused on information about Austria. *Austria-Forum* combines encyclopedic, external resources and user-generated articles.

---

[30] http://www.austriaforum.org, accessed 2008-02-26

Chapter 3 Technology-Enhanced Learning and Teaching

Since the early learning machines, like Ramelli's *book wheel* of 1588 [Lipson, 2008], and much later Bush's *memex* [Bush, 1945], technology has played a part in the acquisition and transfer of knowledge. In the era of modern information and communication technologies (ICT), this role has become increasingly prominent. Technology is applied for didactical, pedagogical, and management purposes. The subsequent pages offer a short introduction into the topics of e-learning, technology-enhanced learning and e-learning 2.0. It is provided as a foundation for the understanding of the subsequent parts of this book, and to ensure a common vocabulary.

3.1 Introduction

Numerous concepts have been used to describe the conjunction of education and technology, though no indisputable definitions for these concepts exist. All concepts at this contact point share the idea to enhance and improve knowledge transfer and knowledge acquisition. In the context of this book the application of ICT to enhance or enable knowledge acquisition and knowledge transfer is denoted by the two terms e-learning and technology-enhanced learning. For the remainder of this work the following definitions should be considered.

Knowledge transfer is the shift of knowledge between individuals or organizations. It may be achieved in communication from human beings to human beings, computer systems to computer systems or computer systems to human beings. All forms of teaching and learning are summarized in this concept.

Knowledge acquisition is seen as the process of capturing knowledge that already exists, for example in an expert or a teacher. In knowledge management, it is used to extend or construct a knowledge model in a knowledge base. Knowledge acquisition can be identified as a process of modeling tasks and domains, and contextualizing of information.

E-learning (electronic learning) encompasses all educational scenarios based on the application of ICT. This includes *distance learning,* where education is provided for students being off-site, or *computer-based training (CBT),* which are self-organized learning activities. In the context of this book, the term e-learning is restricted to teaching and learning heavily or thoroughly relying on the application of ICT.

Technology-enhanced Learning (TEL) in contrast encompasses a broader set of situations. The term describes the application of technology to assist in all kinds of learning practices. As such, technology-enhanced learning ranges from the application of technology in a classroom scenario to a purely Web-based e-learning scenario for informal learning. In contrast to e-learning, teaching must not solemnly occur based on ICT. Moreover, technology-enhanced learning also encompasses the application of ICT without influence on the learning result, like course or content management [Schmees, 2006].

3.2 The Evolution of Technology-Enhanced Learning

Computer- and Web-based educational approaches have been accompanying pedagogical development for several years. The focus in these years has changed from a technology driven development to a pedagogically driven development. Within recent years this evolution has strongly favored socially and communication oriented approaches.

3.2.1 Computer- and Web-Based Training

Right from it's beginning, the Internet in general and the WWW in particular have been applied to various pedagogical systems. The radical idea of a "learning web" has already been introduced in 1971 by the Austrian philosopher Ivan Illich [Illich, 1971], even when there was no suiting technology to support it. He envisioned a decentralized and society driven learning approach where the learner controls the learning process. The first conceptual component of this unconventional learning substitute termed as "learning web", is to provide reference services to educational objects. These services provide the means of access to formal learning material available in institutes, libraries, laboratories etc. at any time and any place. The second component is described as skill exchanges where learners can communicate with instructors about the terms of skill exchange. The third component, peer matching, is a collaborative learning space for learner-learner or learner-instructor activity. The fourth component of this new learning model is to provide reference services to educators at large, which serves as a linkage between numerous learning web segments. Such a network allows a greater wealth of knowledge space and broader access to learning services.

The Web based alternative to conventional learning started as a simple document sharing system, which allowed more open access to educational contents. The pedagogical systems in the early days of the Web came in the form of university Web sites, online file archives, digital libraries, and basic content management systems. Over the years, these Web-based learning environments evolved into more interactive systems supported by rich media technologies. The second breed of pedagogical systems followed a more active learning approach and added interactivity between learner and instructor in form of mail exchange, active messaging and live conferencing.

The more recent World Wide Web emphasizes and facilitates collaboration and knowledge sharing among users introduced the use of social tools in learning environments in form of blogs, wikis and peer-to-peer media sharing services [Safran et al., 2007b]. Concepts of Web 2.0 significantly influenced Web-based learning environments and many learning applications incorporated these ideas. It allowed rich opportunities of user dominated networking and collaborative creation of learning content and structures.

According to a survey about quality and extent of online education in United States [Allen and Seaman, 2004] virtually all public institutes offer some form of online education. Similar trends of complete online or blended/hybrid learning with an emphasis on web based LMS can be seen in Canada, Europe and Australia. 2006/07 campus computing surveys [Green, 2006; Green, 2007] show that more and more higher education institutes are switching to open source Web LMS such as Moodle[31] and Sakai[32]. This can be seen as a step towards standardization of Web learning experience on a larger scale. Deployment of such systems enables collaborative interaction at learner, instructor, institution and system level.

The inherent data intensive nature of learning systems and growing number of users can cause scalability issues. We are yet to see an ideal web based learning environment that supports all pedagogical, information and communication characteristics in a scalable manner. On the next pages, we will review different aspects of scalable web based learning environments with a focus on horizontal scalability of systems.

3.2.1.1 Characteristics of modern learning systems

The effectiveness of a Web-based learning platform depends on its compliance to accepted pedagogical norms as well as its abilities of information representation and exchange. According to a survey [Mioduser et al., 1999] of 436 education websites; very few sites conforms to pedagogical approaches of collaborative learning, active involvement of students with peers and instructors in content building. A look at very recent web based learning environments [EduTools, 2009] in use reveals that there is significant improvement. Newer systems are more pedagogy driven, with possibilities of learner being in control of learning processes. Compared to previous applications cognitive processes are not restricted to information retrieval and memorizing, we see

---

[31] http://moodle.org/, accessed 2010-02-18
[32] http://sakaiproject.org/, accessed 2010-02-18

more possibilities of creation, analysis and inference. Structure and presentation of knowledge is also growing and changing rapidly.

Apart from characteristics coming from web 2.0 some of the desirable features of a modern web based learning system include

- Broader and convenient access to high quality intellectual contents (internal/external)
- Complete control over learning processes management
- Data management, assignments, contents files transfer etc.
- New means of active and passive communication among instructors, learners and external experts
- Support for blended learning, lab experience and simulation.
- Conventional and unconventional evaluation techniques
- Convergence: anywhere any time availability and support for multiple modes of interaction
- Support for learner modeling and personalization
- Centralized tracking and administration features, added support for instructors.
- Intellectual Property Right (IPR) protection, plagiarism checks
- Scalability and interoperability

A number of pedagogical web applications containing subsets of these characteristics exist, but none that covers all aspects or outlined characteristics. Implementation of an ideal web based learning environment requires a seamless integration of such systems that cover all aspects of e-Learning.

3.3 From E-Learning to E-Learning 2.0

The evolution of *Web 2.0* did not only mark a shift in the usage of the Web, but also in society, and, subsequently, in education. In the subset of e-learning this shift was been denoted the term *e-learning 2.0*. This term describes a set of technologies and concepts applied to contemporary e-learning and technology-enhanced learning.

Within the last decades, our society has changed from a product-oriented economy to a service-oriented and knowledge-centered economy. Therefore, employees' knowledge and competences need to be adapted adequately. Consequently, educational goals have also changed significantly, as outlined in [Bransford et al., 2002]. Our modern, knowledge-based society expects much more from students and teachers than ever before. Various learning and teaching styles have become increasingly important; see for example [Ramsay and Ransley, 1986] and [Riding, 1997]. Learning experiences in modern learning processes include collaborative aspects and active contributions to learning content. In order to enable contextualized learning, the provision of additional pre-existing content supports students to link newly acquired knowledge to already well-known problem domains. Moreover, the integration of students' and teachers' preferred tools and platforms into a tailored learning process has become increasingly interesting, as for example outlined in [Gütl, 2008] and [Helic, 2007].

In general, a great variety of information and communication technologies (ICT) can foster above stated learning activities in many ways, such as technical support in traditional learning or in e-learning, see [Bransford et al., 2002] and [Oblinger and Oblinger, 2005]. By focusing on Web-based technologies, comparable to the changes outlined in the paragraph above, the World Wide Web has changed since its invention in 1989 from static to a highly dynamic media in the recent years. In 2005 Tim O'Reilly has coined the term "Web 2.0" for collaborative, user-centric content production and interactive content access [O'Reilly, 2005]. In literature Web 2.0 includes (1) social phenomena such as the Web for participation, (2) technology for significant change in web usage, and (3) design guidelines for loosely coupled services. As in many other application domains, Web 2.0 has also merged into the e-learning domain; see for example [Alexander, 2006]. The application of the Web 2.0 idea in both e-learning technology and methodology is denoted as e-learning 2.0 by Stephen Downes, see [Downes, 2005].

The aim of this chapter is to give a consolidated review on how the concept of Web 2.0 has influenced e-learning. The remainder of this chapter is organized as follows: First of all a number of those Web 2.0 concepts, which impact E-Leaning 2.0, are explained. In the next part, the application of these principles in tangible implementations is presented. In a final step, the impact of e-learning 2.0 concepts on learning is examined by taking a closer look at related surveys. Finally, the conclusions are summarized.

3.3.1 Web 2.0 Concepts and Technology for Learning Activities

The observed change of e-learning from medium to a platform [Downes, 2005] leads to the fact that several Web 2.0 concepts and technologies take influence on contemporary e-learning. On the one hand, there are several core technologies, which are likewise associated with Web 2.0 and e-learning 2.0. On the other hand, the important role of social interaction and collaborative work results in online community applications, this must be considered in the context of learning.

3.3.1.1 Technological Viewpoint

As far as the technological viewpoint is concerned, several points of intersection between e-learning practices and Web 2.0 philosophy can be identified. For each of these points of intersection corresponding Web 2.0 technologies will be recapitulated in this section.

First, there are e-learning approaches, which support communities of practice, i.e. socio-constructivist pedagogical strategy where learners interact and learn together. Interaction typically occurs through discussion, commenting, collaborative writing, or working together on projects [Ocker, 2001; Strijker and Collis, 2002]. Recently, tools such as wikis are being used to support such community aspects in e-learning [Fucks-Kittowski et al., 2004].

Wikis are a technology introduced by Leuf and Cunningham in 1995 [Leuf and Cunningham, 2001]. The term itself is derived from the Hawaiian word wikiwiki, meaning *quick*. The technology is designed to provide a simple tool for knowledge management. Wikis allow all users to create and edit content online. All changes can be retraced by the other users and older versions of documents are available in a revision history. As such, wikis are an easy to use application for collaboratively creating content.

Wikipedia is the best-known wiki system. Originating from the Nupedia project it provides a large online encyclopedia with all of its content published under the GNU free Documentation License or similar. It consists of more than 4 million articles, which are provided in more than 190 languages, with the English version being the largest one. Around 10.000 of Wikipedia's users regularly edit or contribute content [Voss, 2005]. Due to its popularity, Wikipedia has become a popular source in the search for information.

Secondly, some approaches involve learners in the direct process of production of learning content. This notion is one of the most outstanding changes from more learning object oriented approaches. Typically, these approaches are based on tools such as weblogs and podcasts. [Downes, 2005]

A weblog, or blog, is a "log of the web", a term coined by Barger in 1997 [Paquet, 2003]. The key feature of a blog is the presentation of the content in reverse chronological order. Blog software usually provides the possibility for comments and trackbacks, links back from other sites. In such a way, a distributed, collective and interlinked *blogosphere* is created. While wikis are used for collaborative work, blogs are a personal form of publishing content. As far as the educational benefit is concerned a number of possible uses can be identified [Richardson, 2006]. These are:

⊕ Promote critical and analytical thinking

⊕ Promote creative, intuitive and associational thinking

⊕ Promote analogical thinking

⊕ Provide potential for increased access

⊕ Expose to quality information, and have combination of solitary and social interaction.

A podcast is "audio content available on the Internet that can be automatically delivered to your computer or MP3 player" [Geoghengan and Klass, 2005]. In the meantime, the delivery of video with the same technology as a video-podcast or vodcast has also become usual. As far as education is concerned, this technology can be used to deliver course content or course recordings to students. Apple implemented the iTunes U[33] in its iTunes Store, which provides access to lecture recordings from several large universities. The Graz University of Technology likewise provides recordings of several large lectures for its students [Ebner, 2007].

The basic technology of podcasting and a feature of most blog software is RSS. The abbreviation stands for "Rich Site Summary" or "Real Simple Syndication". The technology allows the user to subscribe to a regular news update of a site and thus receive information on new content in a push approach rather than scanning for changes manually. The RSS information available on such a site is called RSS feed [Duffy and Bruns, 2006]. In education, the students might syndicate their content by using for example RSS feeds. [Anido, 2006]

Lastly there are approaches such as e-portfolio where learners have their own place to create, reflect on and showcase their work [Downes, 2005]. Systems like ELGG[34] provide a possibility for students to present themselves and their ability.

---

[33] http://www.apple.com/education/itunesu/, accessed 2009-04-20
[34] http://elgg.org/, accessed 2009-04-20

Chapter 3

3.3.1.2 Social Aspects

While e-learning initially was much focused on the content the social interaction, assisting informal learning, has gained an important role. Instead of a limitation of social interaction on topics for a given course, interaction with students worldwide on a wide range of topics has become usual [Downes, 2005]. While social aspects of existing e-learning software as for example messaging and forums are still important, other possibilities also require consideration.

Several online community sites like Facebook[35] or StudiVZ[36] focus on articulating social networks and the interlinking of users. StudiVZ especially targets as students as users and, for example, offers the possibility to find other students enrolled to the same lectures.

Another aspect of Web 2.0 concepts interesting in the context of e-learning are Web sharing applications [Ebner, 2007]. On the one hand, this involves social bookmarking tools like del.icio.us[37], which allow users to share their bookmarks and tag websites. On the other hand, media sharing like Flickr[38] or Youtube[39] provide the possibility to share multimedia files. Beside the more general use of this system, the use for course related content is also possible.

3.3.2 E-learning 2.0 Examples

As stated above, the majority of Web 2.0 applications encourage active user participation in creating, sharing and structuring data. In particular, collaboration and social interactions between the users are the basic means supported by modern Web 2.0 applications to meet these goals. Although the definition of the term "Web 2.0" [O'Reilly, 2005] concisely summarized the basic design principles and motivation

---

[35] http://www.facebook.com/, accessed 2009-04-20
[36] http://www.studivz.net/, accessed 2009-04-20
[37] http://del.icio.us/, accessed 2009-04-20
[38] http://www.flickr.com/, accessed 2009-04-20
[39] http://www.youtube.com/, accessed 2009-04-20

behind the Web 2.0 movement, there have been numerous attempts in the past to follow similar approaches in implementing e-learning tools – for instance, to support users in collaborative creation of learning content and structures. In this chapter, two such examples - dating back two years before the initial definition of "Web 2.0" - are shortly presented. The examples have been developed at IICM as a part of the WBT-Master system [Helic et al., 2004c].

The first example is a tool called Virtual Project-Management Room that supports so-called project-based pedagogical approach where learners work on real-life projects [Helic et al., 2005]. Typically, projects are complex tasks, based on challenging questions or problems, which involve learners in design, problem-solving, decision-making, investigative activities, and culminate in realistic products or presentations. Other defining features found of project-based learning paradigm include authentic content, authentic assessment, teacher facilitation but not direction, explicit educational goals, cooperative and collaborative learning, and reflection. The developed tool integrated the following components into a single tool to meet such sophisticated pedagogical requirements:

- Description the course and project motivation, problems that need to be solved, goals, etc.

- Discussion folder providing a sample project with the definition of project plan, e.g. number of project steps and the timetable for these steps.

- A number of project discussion folders, which provide project alternatives for learners to choose. These folders hold also all learner contributions.

- A number of collaboration and communication tools, such as online presence lists, chat rooms, annotation tools, discussion forums, etc.

- Evaluation tool for teachers evaluating learners' work.

In principles, learners are supposed to be acquainted with the sample project in order to learn about the project plan and the steps they need to accomplish. After that, the learners work in small groups by following the project plan. Typically, each project step requires that learners create content in collaboration, share that content with the group members and/or with other learner groups. Additionally, the content might be annotated or commented by other learners facilitating in this very important discussion about the course topics, the task at hand, and the user-created content itself. To ensure that learners' work stays focused the teacher monitors the progress and provides guidance if needed.

The second example deals with enriching of discussion contributions with structured metadata to improve information retrieval possibilities in educational discussion forums [Helic et al., 2004a]. Discussion boards have been recognized in e-learning not only as a means for asynchronous communication but also as a tool to collaboratively create content and as a tool for experts' knowledge extraction. However, searching for a particular contribution or navigating to a specific thread of discussion is typically tedious and time-consuming task.

Therefore, a tool has been developed that allows users to structure the contributions from a discussion forum in a collaborative manner, i.e. by assigning contributions to one or more categories from a predefined taxonomy. To leverage collective interactions a voting mechanism has been implemented. Thus, whenever a contribution is assigned to a particular category the users can vote on that assignment, i.e. they can vote "pro" or "contra" that assignment. If an assignment gets more "contra" votes than the contribution is removed from that category. Otherwise, the number of "pro" votes is a simple "collective" measure of a particular contribution belonging to a specific category (see Figure 3-1).

The category structure and the contribution assignments are than utilized to improve search and navigation facilities. In addition, the predefined taxonomy might be altered on-the-fly, i.e. the taxonomy is flexible in the sense that it can be extended, the categories can be modified and deleted by the users of the system. In a sense, it is a similar approach to the concept of "folksonomies". The difference is the top-down approach (a session is started with a predefined taxonomy) and the relations between categories are always hierarchical.

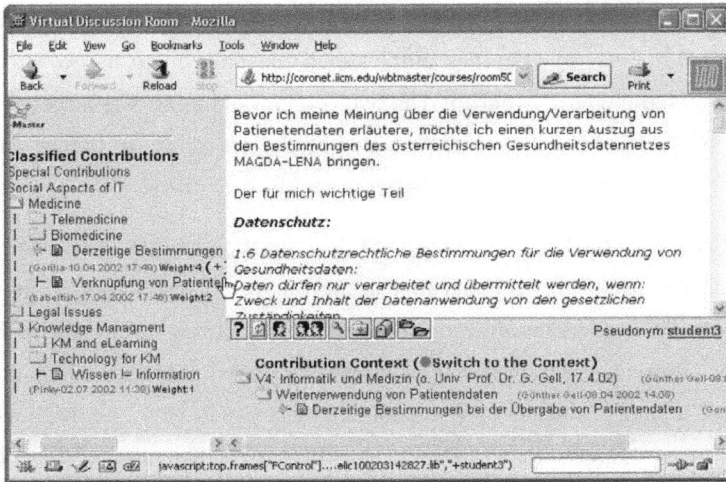

Figure 3-1: Voting mechanism for classification of contributions [Helic et al., 2004a].

3.3.3 E-learning 2.0: Hype or another Bubble

Having taken a closer look at the basic principles and some examples of e-learning 2.0 it is necessary to consider the impact that these concepts have on learning today. Several experts predict further rise in the importance of collaboratively created content and other Web 2.0 concepts in the context of e-learning for 2007 [Neal, 2007]. The most interesting question is, however, to what extent the technologies and concepts of e-learning 2.0 are already used in learning environments.

Generally, the knowledge about Web 2.0 and its concepts seems to be still relatively low in the general population. A survey by the PR Agency ZPR[40] showed that only 6% of the Germans aged between 16 and 65 know the term *Web 2.0*. 16% are member of an online community, 14% use podcasts and only 9% read weblogs regularly. The results where higher for those users aged 16 to 20, in which case 42% are member of an online community and 35% read weblogs regularly.

---

[40] http://www.z-pr.de/images/downloads/zpr/061102_umfrage_web_2.0_pm.pdf, accessed 2009-04-20

A more detailed online survey conducted by the University of Oxford [White, 2007] from December 2006 to February 2007 aimed to analyze the use of online tools associated with the Web 2.0 concept. The two versions of this survey targeted students on the suite of online short courses provided by the University of Oxford on the one hand and academics teaching in weekly classes on the other hand.

The survey covered the levels of usage and the application area of social bookmarking, calendaring, image sharing, collaborative authoring, video sharing, social networking, weblogs, file sharing, communication tools and social games / spaces distributed by age groups. Interesting features in the context of e-learning 2.0 is the high number of people from all age groups using Wikipedia being between 70% and 80%, while only at about 20% of the participates stated to use other wikis. The number of people using social bookmarking is quite low with the highest amount of people being under 18 years of age. Weblogs are read by 50-60% of the participants from all age groups, while only a larger number of the under 18 year old and 18 to 24 year old participants write their own weblogs. A similar distribution can be seen for the use of social networking tools.

As far as the application area is concerned, the most interesting one in the context of this chapter is the use for study. Wikipedia and Discussion Forums are the only two applications, which are used to a large degree for study purposes. Other applications, which are at least to some extent used for study purposes are weblogs, wikis, MSN Messenger and calendaring software.

A related survey was conducted at the IICM aiming to analyze the use of Web 2.0 applications privately and for learning, taking into account the familiarity with Web technologies. The survey was conducted in June 2007 and was targeted on the participants of one computer science course in the first and one in the third year of the bachelor program as well as one course for master level students.

In a first part of the survey the technical background knowledge and the familiarity with several Web technologies was asked for. In the second part of the survey the basic knowledge about and the frequency of use of several Web 2.0 applications was covered. The applications in question are weblogs, wikis, audio-podcasts, video-podcasts, mashups, social bookmarking, social networks, media sharing tools and virtual worlds. The results of this survey are presented in Chapter 4.

3.3.4 Conclusions and Summary

In the wake of Web 2.0, an adequate concept called e-learning 2.0 has been denoted. These two concepts show many points of intersection, as several of the core applications associated to Web 2.0 are also important in e-learning 2.0. On the one hand, modern e-learning systems implement several of these aspects already. On the other hand, surveys showed that several parts of Web 2.0 are still only used by a minority of students.

This fact has several implications. First of all the most important influence seems to emanate on the one side from Wikipedia respectively wikis in general and on the other side from blogs. Yet this also means that other applications still lack the importance on e-learning that has been predicted. One reason may be that the age group most proficient with these technologies has not yet reached the university level, which both surveys aimed for as far as the participants are concerned. Another reason could be that there is still a long way to go in finding useful possibilities to integrate these applications in e-learning.

Chapter 4 The Initial Situation at Universities

In the recent years there has been a lot of discussion about technologies and applications labeled "Web 2.0" and its influence on technology-enhanced learning. "Web 2.0", labeling an idea rather than a concrete technology, lead to the definition of the related concept "e-learning 2.0" and research on the application of corresponding online tools and technologies in technology-enhanced learning has been published. Yet, the actual inclusion of such concepts in everyday learning situations, especially in university settings, remained undetermined for some time. This chapter describes the analysis of a survey conducted to verify the influence of "Web 2.0" applications for learning at the Graz University of Technology conducted in 2006. The goal was to investigate the frequency of passive use, work as a developer and use in lectures and learning, as well as the influence of the education level thereon. The survey was released to students of lectures ranging from first-year to master students.

4.1.1 Introduction

Since the first Web 2.0 conference in 2004 and even more since the well-known article by Tim O'Reilly [O'Reilly, 2005] defining this term, there has been a lot of controversy and discussion in the scientific community about this topic. Undoubtedly there has been a change in the way the web has been used in the last years, from a primarily passive to a largely participative way. Rather than describing certain technologies, "Web 2.0" can be seen as an idea comprising individual production and user generated content, harnessing the power of the crowd, data on an epic scale, architecture of participation, network effects and openness [Anderson, 2007]. In the wake of this discussion and the hype in the media, a lot of more or less new applications and technologies have been associated with the term Web 2.0. The ensuing paradigm shift largely moves teacher and student to collaborative learning and the application of Web

2.0 related technologies like weblogs, and wikis in technology-enhanced learning lead to the concept of "E-learning 2.0" [Downes, 2005].

In [Raitman and Augar, 2005], for example, the application of wikis for online collaboration in tertiary education environment is described and a case study was evaluated. Other applications that are proposed for the use in e-learning are blogs and podcasts. Universities like the Graz University of Technology offer such services to their students[41] and several teachers include the use of online tools in their courses. One of these services is the providing of lecture recordings as video podcasts [Ebner et al., 2007].

Yet the question, to what extend such offers are used by the students, remained largely open for some time, although a survey at the University of Oxford is described in [White, 2007], which tried to answer this question. This survey contained questions concerning the types of usage of different online tools, which share the "Web 2.0" label. The survey results contained little analysis, offering possibilities for the readers to interpret the numbers themselves. This motivated us to make a survey at the Graz University of Technology investigating the extent and type of usage of Web 2.0 applications in a university environment.

4.1.2 Web 2.0 Usage Survey

In order to find comparable numbers for the situation at the Graz University of Technology as well as to gain additional insights' a survey was designed. The first objective of this survey was to verify the level of usage of different technologies associated with the concept "Web 2.0". This concerned the passive usage as well as the active development of applications or websites.

The second objective was comparable to the survey described in [White, 2007]. It was to verify the level of usage of different types of Web 2.0 applications. While

---

41   http://tugll.tugraz.at/, accessed 2009-04-22

aforementioned survey discerned the types of usage into social use, use for study, and use for work, we decided to allow separate frequencies for the categories passive use as a consumer, active use as an author or contributor, use in lectures guided by a teacher or use in learning situations of one's own accord.

The survey was designed for the students of three different lectures. The first lecture was for first year students, while the second one was for students at the end of their bachelor program. The final lecture involved was for students in their master program. The vast majority of the participants of these lectures study Computer Science, Telematics, Software Development-Economics, Technical Mathematics, or Biomedical Engineering.

Beside the basic statistics describing the knowledge and the usage frequency of the participants, it was aimed to verify a number of hypotheses concerning the correlations of some of the survey's variables. Table 4-1 depicts the details on these hypotheses.

The first set of hypotheses concerned the influence of the academic education, presented by the lecture attended, which roughly equaled the year in the curriculum. A second set of hypotheses was focused on two derived variables. *Familiarity* summarizes the frequencies of the passive usage of the observed technologies. *Proficiency* summarizes the frequencies of development with these technologies. These hypotheses were tested by calculating the Pearson's correlation coefficients for the variables concerned and verifying the significance with a Student's t-test at a confidence level of 0.95.

4.1.3 Detailed Survey Setup

Matching the objectives of the survey, it was split into three parts. The first part covered demographic information about the participants. The second part covered a list of technologies associated with the term Web 2.0. Finally the third part covered applications associated with Web 2.0. Only the most basic questions in the demographic part were compulsory to be answered.

The demographic part of the survey covered the gender and the age as basic information. Moreover details to the participants' studies were requested; being the type of curriculum, the year in curriculum, and which of the three lectures had been visited.

Table 4-1: Hypotheses for Web 2.0 usage at Universities

H_1	Advanced students know more about technologies associated with Web 2.0.
H_2	Advanced students use such technologies more frequently.
H_3	Advanced students develop applications with such technologies more frequently.
H_4	Advanced students know more about applications associated with Web 2.0.
H_5	Advanced students use such applications more frequently.
H_6	Advanced students provide content in such applications more frequently.
H_7	Advanced students have used such applications in courses more frequently
H_8	Advanced students use such applications in learning more frequently.
H_9	Advanced students have gained a higher familiarity with Web 2.0 technologies.
H_{10}	Advanced students have gained a higher proficiency with Web 2.0 technologies.

H_{11}	Students, who have higher familiarity rating, know more about applications associated with Web 2.0.
H_{12}	Students, who have higher familiarity rating, use such applications more frequently.
H_{13}	Students, who have higher familiarity rating, provide content in such applications more frequently.
H_{14}	Students, who have higher familiarity rating, use such applications in learning more frequently.
H_{15}	Students, who have higher proficiency rating, know more about applications associated with Web 2.0.
H_{16}	Students, who have higher proficiency rating, use such applications more frequently.
H_{17}	Students, who have higher proficiency rating, provide content in such applications more frequently.
H_{18}	Students, who have higher proficiency rating, use such applications in learning more frequently.

The target of the technologies section was to measure the level of proficiency the students have in a number of web technologies. To that end, after checking the basic knowledge about these technologies, two levels of proficiency were of interest. The first level was whether the participant uses the technology passively as a user. The second one was whether he uses it actively as a developer. For both of these levels the frequency of use was asked for, from never to daily. The technologies covered were Really Simple Syndication (RSS) feeds, Asynchronous JavaScript and XML (AJAX), Service Oriented Architecture Protocol (SOAP), Representational State Transfer (REST), podcasts, wiki software, and weblog software.

The final part of the survey was designed to learn about the usage of several of those applications, which are summarized to the term Web 2.0 and are interesting in the context of technology-enhanced learning. After checking basic knowledge about these applications, the frequency of usage in four different levels was asked for. These four levels were passive usage like reading, active usage meaning the providing of content, guided usage as part of a university lecture, and individual usage during learning. Finally, the participants were asked to sort the applications by their importance for collaborative respectively individual learning and were asked to name examples for the application types, which they used. A first group of applications, which represented applications used in the course of e-learning activities at the Graz University of Technology, consisted of weblogs, wikis, audio-podcasts, and video-podcasts. A second group consisted of other Web 2.0 applications, being mashups, social bookmarking, social networks, media sharing, and virtual realities.

4.1.4 Results

183 of the 831 participants of the three lectures involved completed the survey, resulting in a rate of return of 22%. 90.71% of these were male, matching the gender distribution of the involved course programs. The majority of 69.95% of the participants are aged between 21 and 25 years. 42.62% of the participants study Telematics, and 34.98% Software Development-Economy, while the remaining students are spread over the other possible course programs. 68.31% of the participants were students of the first-year lecture, 21.31% attended the lecture at the end of the bachelor programs, and 16.94% the master program lecture.

4.1.4.1 Technologies

The basic analysis of the answers in the technology part of the survey yielded the result that wikis, weblogs, podcasts, and RSS feeds were best known, as shown in Table 4-2. The other technologies in question were far less known amongst the participants. While this was presumed for SOAP and REST, the fact that the concepts of

AJAX and tag clouds were only known to a small number of students came as a surprise.

Table 4-2: Knowledge about Technologies

	RSS	AJAX	SOAP	REST
Known	74,3%	42,1%	21,3%	4,4%
Unknown	12,0%	36,1%	60,7%	75,4%
Not Sure	10,9%	15,8%	12,0%	9,8%
No Answer	2,7%	6,0%	6,0%	10,4%

	Pod-cast	Wiki	Weblog	Tag Cloud
Known	73,2%	95,1%	80,9%	18,6%
Unknown	7,7%	2,2%	7,7%	61,2%
Not Sure	14,8%	2,2%	9,3%	12,0%
No Answer	4,4%	0,5%	2,2%	8,2%

Subsequently the figures were investigated in correlation to the lecture visited by the participants. This showed that while the technologies AJAX, SOAP, REST and tag clouds were less well known by the first year students, they were better known by the master level students. Table 4-3 gives a detailed overview on the knowledge about the individual technologies. This difference was especially outstanding for AJAX, which was known by only 29.57% of the first year students but by 90.32% of the master level students.

Table 4-3: Distribution of "Technology Known"

	RSS	AJAX	SOAP	REST	Pod-cast	Wiki	Web-log	Tag Cloud
First year	69,2 %	29,6 %	13,7 %	1,8%	72,0 %	93,6 %	76,0 %	9,7%
Bachelor	87,2 %	52,6 %	24,3 %	6,3%	84,6 %	100 %	94,9 %	34,3 %
Master	87,1 %	90,3 %	53,3 %	16,7 %	83,3 %	100 %	96,8 %	41,9 %

The analysis of the passive and active use frequencies of these technologies yielded the result that only wikis were used very often. Weblogs and RSS were used at quite often, with 51% respectively 40% of the participants using them at least on a weekly basis. More than 50% of the participants stated that they never use AJAX, SOAP, REST and tag clouds. Figure 4-1 shows the complete distribution auf the frequencies of use.

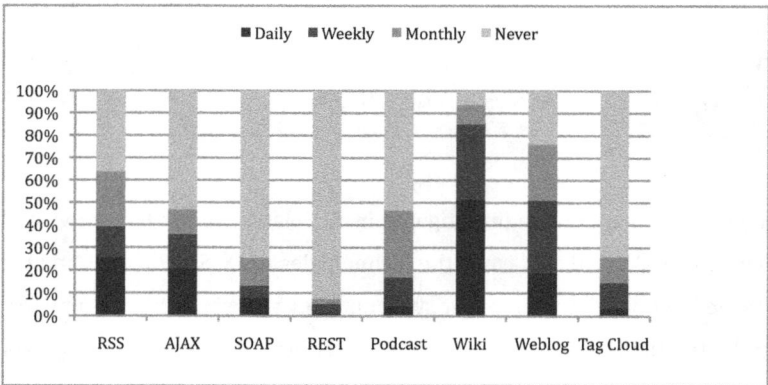

Figure 4-1: Use Frequency of Technologies

The statistic for the frequency of development for the eight technologies resembles these trends. Wikis, weblogs and RSS were used most often, while the other technologies were almost never used. Figure 4-2 details this distribution.

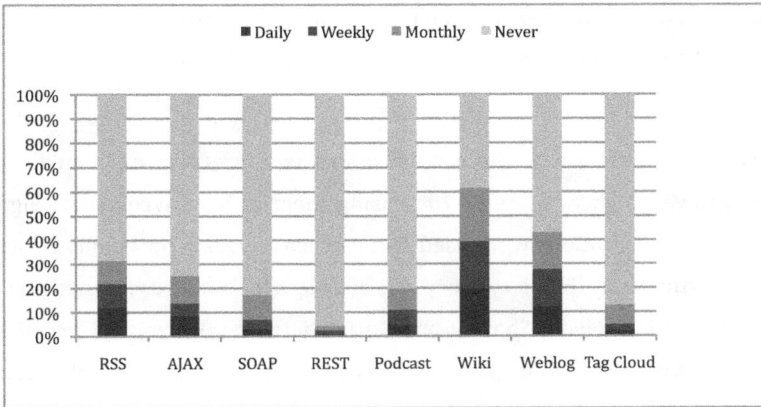

Figure 4-2: Development Frequency with Technologies

Investigating the correlations of advance in curriculum and knowledge about the eight technologies yielded significant correlations of 0.19 for RSS, 0.46 for AJAX, 0.37 for SOAP, 0.34 for REST, 0.26 for weblogs and 0.32 for tag clouds. For these technologies H_1 can be confirmed. There is only a high correlation for AJAX, and a medium correlation for SOAP, REST and tag clouds.

As far as the use frequency is concerned, significant correlations could be found for RSS, AJAX, SOAP, wikis, weblogs and tag clouds. All of these correlations are between 0.23 and 0.27, being rather low. For these technologies, H_2 can be confirmed, although there is a low connection. The correlation of advance in the curriculum and the derived variable *familiarity* is also significant, at a medium 0.36. H_9 can be confirmed.

The investigation of the correlation with development frequency yielded significant results for RSS, AJAX, SOAP, wikis and tag clouds. Again, the correlation was rather low to medium, ranging from 0.18 to 0.30. For these five technologies, H_3 can be confirmed. The correlation for the derived variable *proficiency* was also significant and at 0.29. H_{10} also can be confirmed.

4.1.4.2 Applications

Table 4-4 shows the results of the basic analysis of knowledge about the Web 2.0 applications. Both most common types, podcasts and media sharing platforms, were known by most participants. More than 60% of the participants knew about mashups. Only about 40% of the participants knew about social bookmarking and social networks.

As far as the passive use of these applications is concerned, only media sharing platforms showed high rates, with 70% using them at least weekly. As Figure 4-3 shows, all other applications were used on an at least weekly basis only by less than 30% of the participants. This frequency was even less for active use providing content, as Figure 4-4 shows. Media Sharing and Social Networks were used on an at least weekly basis only by 30% of the participants, while all other types of applications were used even less often.

Table 4-4: Knowledge of Applications

	Audio-Podcasts	Video-Podcasts	Mash ups	Social Book-marking	Social Networks	Media Sharing
Known	82,0%	78,1%	62,8%	36,1%	41,0%	91,8%
Unknown	5,5%	5,5%	17,5%	38,3%	31,7%	1,1%
Not Sure	7,7%	12,6%	15,8%	16,4%	16,4%	3,3%
No Answer	4,9%	3,8%	3,8%	9,3%	10,9%	3,8%

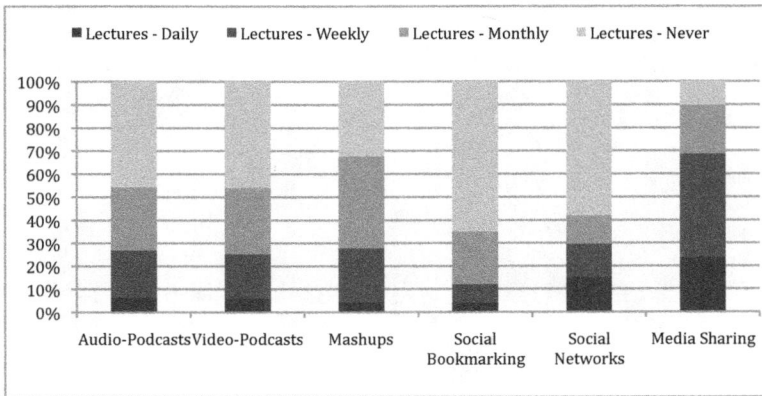

Figure 4-3: Use Frequency for Applications

The investigation on the use in lectures (guided use) or the use in learning (individual use) of these 6 applications, as well as wikis, weblogs and virtual worlds showed that only wikis and weblogs were used regularly by a significant number of the participants. Wikis were used in the course of lectures by 60% on an at least weekly basis, for individual learning even by 84%. Weblogs were used at least weekly by 20% in lectures and 30% while learning. As Figure 4-5 shows, all other applications were rarely used in the course of lectures, with virtual worlds not being used by 99% of the participants. Figure 4-6 shows that these applications were also rarely used in individual learning.

This trend was also reflected in the ranking of applications the participants were asked to do. When ranking the nine applications by the importance for collaborative learning 84.7% of the participants replied that wikis are most important. As second most important application, weblogs were chosen by 38.8%. As far as the importance for individual learning is concerned, 88.52% chose wikis as the most important application and 44.26% weblogs as the second most important.

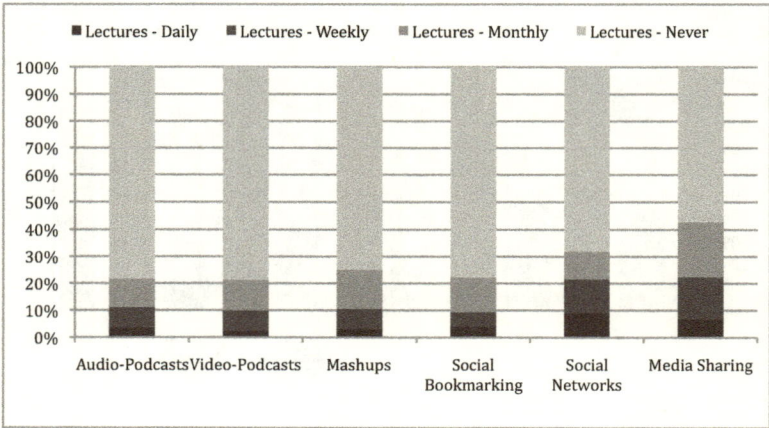

Figure 4-4: Content Providing Frequency for Applications

The investigation of the influence of advance in the curriculum on knowledge and the frequency of use of these applications yielded almost no significant results. The only significant correlation was between the advance in curriculum and the knowledge of social bookmarks, being a medium 0.40. In all other cases, H_4, H_5, H_6, H_7 and H_8 have to be abandoned.

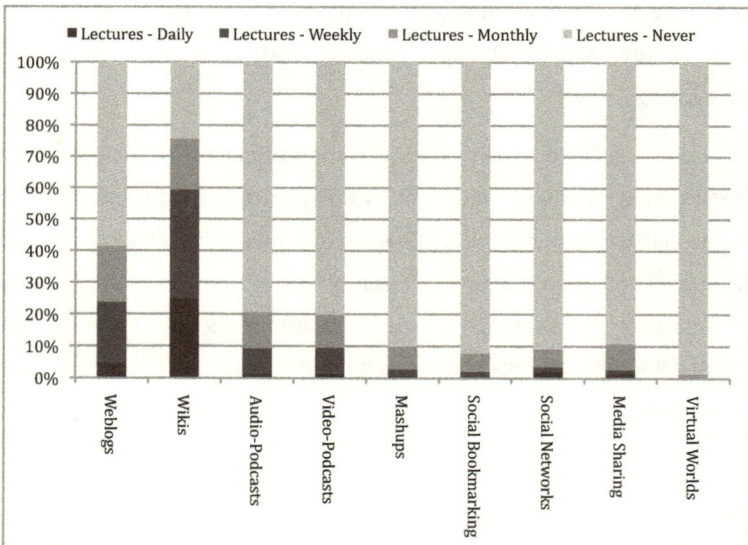

Figure 4-5: Lecture Use Frequency for Applications

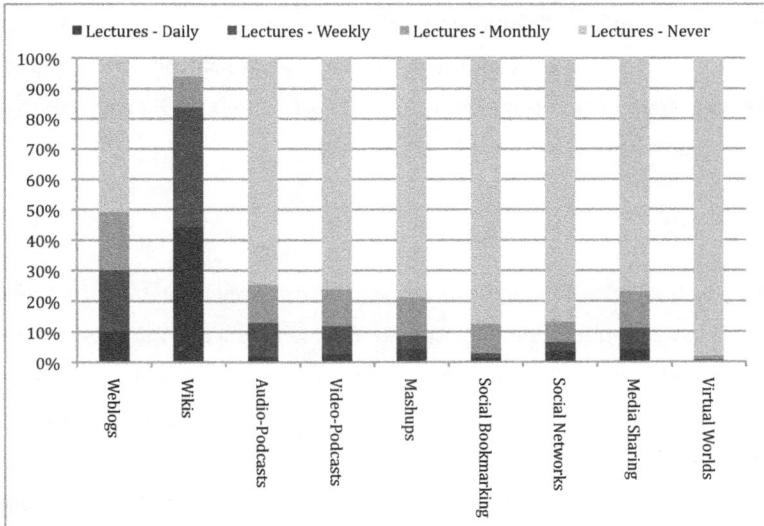

■ Lectures - Daily   ■ Lectures - Weekly   ■ Lectures - Monthly   ▨ Lectures - Never

Weblogs, Wikis, Audio-Podcasts, Video-Podcasts, Mashups, Social Bookmarking, Social Networks, Media Sharing, Virtual Worlds

Figure 4-6: Learning Use Frequency for Applications

The derived variable *familiarity* had a significant correlation of 0.54 and 0.52 with the knowledge of social bookmarks and social networks. H_{11} can be confirmed for these two applications. As far as the use frequency was concerned, familiarity had a significant correlation of 0.40 with audio podcasts and video podcasts, 0.39 with mashups, 0.54 with social bookmarks, 0.47 with social networks and 0.39 with media sharing platforms. H_{12} can be confirmed for all applications. As far as the active use were concerned, there again is only a significant correlation for social bookmarks and social networks, being 0.48 and 0.37 respectively. H_{13} can be confirmed for these two applications. There are no significant correlations for familiarity with the frequency of use in lectures of learning. H_{13} and H_{14} must be abandoned.

Proficiency as the summary of development frequency had no significant correlation with the knowledge of any application. H_{15} must be abandoned. There was a significant correlation to the use frequency of audio podcasts with 0.37, video podcasts with 0.41 and social bookmarks with 0.41. H_{16} can be confirmed for these three applications. As far as the providing of content was concerned, there was a significant correlation of proficiency with audio podcasts (0.46), video podcasts (0.45), mashups (0.45), social bookmarks (0.48), and media sharing (0.46). This means H_{17} must be abandoned for social networks. H_{18} can be confirmed for weblogs, social bookmarks, and social networks, due to significant correlations of 0.42, 0.49 and 0.36. Finally, due to the lack of significant correlations, H_{19} must be abandoned.

4.1.5 Conclusions

Web 2.0, its technologies and applications have become emerging topics within the last years, which have been frequently discussed in mass media and addressed in scores of conferences. Moreover, many information service providers and major vendors in information technology have at least announced Web 2.0 support, and even major industry analyst firms have put their interest on this topic. Despite this hype, our study showed some unexpected results about the knowledge of Web 2.0 technologies and the usage of Web 2.0 applications:

- Computer science students had surprisingly little knowledge about the basic technologies, such as AJAX, SOAP and REST, and consequently they apply these techniques very seldom in their development projects.

- The subjects' interest in Web 2.0 applications given by frequent passive usage and active content contributions was also surprisingly low.

Only media sharing and mashup applications seemed to be well established in our subject group. Given the fact, that Web 2.0 is not another bubble in the new economy, curricula need to be adapted in order to educate students according to industry's needs.

E-learning 2.0 praises interesting and promising concepts by applying Web 2.0 technologies, Web 2.0 applications and their collaborative aspects. This enthusiasm was contrasted by the sobering results of our study. Most of Web 2.0 applications were scarcely used in courses and in self-organized learning activities. Only weblogs and wikis were frequently used Web 2.0 applications in learning processes. The study results reflected that the broad spectrum of Web 2.0 applications was yet not well adopted by teachers at Graz University of Technology, and thus not well presented in courses. Similarly, students seemed not to have adopted Web 2.0 applications for their daily communication and knowledge work, and thus it was not well presented in their self-organized learning activities. In this context, the question rises, why most of technologies and applications were not more frequently used.

This survey was the subjected to two limitations. Firstly, the survey was conducted with an only survey tool, at which only 22% of the potential participants replied. Secondly, the participants were limited to the specific setting of Graz University of Technology. Similar studies with a broader set of participants would be advisable in order to compare them to this setting.

PART II

Scenarios for the Application of Social Media in Higher Education

Chapter 5 Learning by Self Reflection with Weblogs

This chapter describes a case study at the Graz University of Technology on the use of weblogs in a higher education programming course for Computer Science students. Weblogs, as a tool for knowledge sharing, have received plenty of attention in recent years. Due to the support of constructivist learning models, they have also been credited importance in supporting students' learning performance. Several case studies have been conducted showing positive influence on student's success. However, those case studies were based on the fact of introducing weblogs as an obligatory part of coursework for the students. The research presented sought to determine the influence of maintaining a weblog as a personal learning log and e-Portfolio would positively influence the students' performance in a large programming course with the explicit precondition that blogging was voluntary and no necessary part of coursework.

5.1 Weblogs in Higher Education Programming Lectures

In recent years, weblogs have received plenty of attention, due to the fact, that they provide an easy-to-use tool for publication on the Web. The term *weblog* for a "log of the web" has already been coined in 1997 [Paquet, 2003] and basically characterizes a diary-like website that presents entries in reverse chronological order. The fact that plenty of weblog systems are available, which allow easy creation and maintenance of weblogs without technical knowledge as well as additional technologies like *trackbacks* providing added value by interlinking individual blogs added to this technology's popularity.

As far as learning is concerned, weblogs have also been credited plenty of importance. Downes credited the upcoming use of weblogs in education in 2005 [Downes, 2005] as one of the Web technologies stimulating a change in e-learning by supporting collaborative, informal learning. Numerous possible advantages are accredited to weblogs, like the promotion of critical and analytical thinking, as well as creative, intuitive and associational thinking and to provide potential for increased access [Richardson, 2006].

Though all these positive opinions hint at the popularity of weblogs, the adoption rate is still not adequate [White, 2007]. A usage survey at the Graz University of Technology showed similar facts and revealed, that many students lack knowledge about social media in general, and that weblogs find little impact on learning at our university [Safran et al., 2007a].

Programming lectures appear especially well suited for the integration of weblogs as learning logs, in order to foster critical reflection of the own work, as they usually consist of a large practical part and a smaller theoretical part. Increased reflection on the own practical work could result in better understanding of the underlying concepts, and thus better performance in the theoretical part.

In order to verify the positive impact of blogging in such a scenario, a case study has been set up to incorporate weblog usage into a first-year programming lecture in Computer Science curricula. The study was intended to give the students the possibility to write down their learning activities in a weblog and to investigate the relation of weblog activity with the students' performance in the lecture. The total number of students attending the course was 517.

An explicit precondition for this case study was the use of weblogs on a voluntary basis. Therefore, the content of the weblogs was not assessed for the final grade and students, who denied blogging, had the opportunity to stick to alternative assignments. Thus we provided a scenario where the use of weblogs was enabled and encouraged but not compulsory.

5.2 Weblogs in Education

Weblogs in education serve as an enhancement of learning logs, which have already been used some time before weblogs were widely known [Baker, 2003]. Students are encouraged to document their concurrent learning experiences in such a log. The approach is based on the constructivist learning theory, which describes learning as a process of constructing knowledge by an individual [Leidner and Jarvenpaa, 1995]. This process works best when the student is actively engaged in acquiring, generating, analyzing and structuring information [Alavi, 1994].

With the use of weblogs, this didactical concept can be brought into the domain of the Web, where such logs can be written and accessed at any time and from any place. They are used as learning logs, or to form loosely coupled learning networks [Efimova and Fiedler, 2004]. Embedded in personal learning spaces and used in conjunction with e-Portfolios and social networking functionality they can provide a tool to enhance learning [Razavi and Iverson, 2006]. One main advantage is the fact that weblogs foster continuous critical reflection of the own work, prohibiting compact learning by the end of a lecture [Ebner and Maurer, 2007].

Weblogs have been used in individual scenarios for education for some years, with a focus on humanistic and journalism studies [Stanley, 2004], [Wiltse, 2004]. As far as technology education is concerned, earlier studies have shown that the performance in course accompanying blogging can be used as a predictor for the overall performance [Du and Wagner, 2005], [Du and Wagner, 2007].

5.3 Case Study

Six hypotheses were formulated based on the hypotheses of the earlier similar experiments described before, and extended and adapted to the scenario of a programming lecture. These hypotheses are based on the cognitive learning theory described above. They focus on the use of weblogs as a tool to foster critical reflection of the own work and the assumed improvement of the learning process. The first set of hypotheses covers the assumption that this reflection leads to a better understanding of the theoretical concepts underneath the practical programming examples. They are based on a scenario of blogging class, as opposed to a group with standard class and focused work by the end of the class.

⊕ H1: Authoring of weblogs leads to better overall learning performance.

⊕ H2: Authoring of weblogs leads to better improvement during the learning process.

⊕ H3: Authoring of weblogs leads to an improved possibility to transfer practical experience into theoretical knowledge.

⊕ The second set of hypotheses deals with the effect of keeping a weblog on the practical performance itself, as well with the effects of weblogs on fellow students, which are able and encouraged to read their peers' weblogs.

⊕ H4: Participants, who write weblog entries more often, perform better in the practical part of the lecture.

⊕ H5: A given community of participants with a high number of overall postings performs better in the practical part of the lecture.

⊕ H6: A given community of participants with a high number of posters performs better in the practical part of the lecture.

5.3.1 Pre-study Survey

Prior to the beginning of the experiment, the students attending the lecture conducted an online survey to investigate the level of experience with social media and other online tools, both as users and as developers, in order to assess the group of participants. The survey was conducted as an online survey in October 2007. 255 of the participating students completed the survey.

Table 5-1. Use of communication channels

	Never	Rarely	Regularly
E-Mail	0.00%	3.14%	88.63%
Newsgroups	5.10%	21.96%	63.53%
Instant Messaging	11.76%	19.22%	60.00%

The survey consisted of two parts. The first part investigated the participants' demographic background and information about the availability of broadband Internet connection and IT equipment. As far as the latter is concerned, 79.22% of the students owned a laptop, 71.37% owned a desktop PC, 69.03% owned an MP3 player, and 55.69% owned a mobile phone with internet connectivity. The majority of the students have broadband access (73.33%).

The second part of the survey consisted of questions concerning the use of various communication channels and Web applications. The majority of the students use various communication channels regularly as Table 5-1 depicts.

As far as Web applications are concerned, the participants were on the one hand asked whether they act as users or contributors. On the other hand, they were asked whether they used the application on their own accord for learning, or guided by teachers in lectures. 47.06% of the participants use weblogs passively, 15.29% write their own weblog. Only the minority of the participants had been facing weblogs in education. 2.75% of the students have used weblogs in learning, and 4.31% have been guided to use weblogs in lectures. 20.78% of the students have never heard about weblogs before.

Several other web applications were even less well known by the participants. 58.04% of the participants did not know social bookmarking tools, 28.24% were new to podcasts, 34.51% had never heard of virtual worlds before, and to 68.24% of the participants micro-blogging was unknown. Well-known web applications were wikis and social networks. Especially Wikipedia is used for learning by 30.98% of the participants. The Facebook equivalent for German speakers, StudiVZ, was actively used by 74.12%.

The results of the pre-test survey matched the results of the survey in the previous year. Social Web applications were unknown to a large part of the participants and only a minority has been developing Web applications themselves. The most commonly known and used social Web applications were wikis, followed by weblogs. Thus, the use of weblogs in learning was new to a majority of the students.

5.3.2 Experiment Setup

The experiment was conducted during the summer term 2008, from March to June. The participating 517 students were divided into ten groups, each group supported by a mentoring tutor. Five of these groups were offered the standard learning tools for this course (practical examples, tutorials on campus, online documents and screencasts of the lecture). These groups served as comparison groups. The remaining five groups were blogging groups, which formed the test group for the experiment.

Students in these blogging groups could voluntarily create an e-portfolio and blog about their learning progress. As an additional encouragement, the students were offered additional points to the course's regular assessment. These points equaled 5% of the course's total assessment. The only limitations for this bonus were to post at least once every week and to make the posts at least available to their group's community. The content of the posts was at the author's own discretion as long as it was related to the course, the programming language or other topics relevant to the course.

As there should not be any disadvantages for those students not participating in the experiment, they were provided an alternative opportunity to improve their assessment score by an equal amount. This concerned those students from blogging groups, who chose not keep a weblog, as well as the students from the other groups. This alternative bonus was designed to offer a contrast to the ongoing participation during course with a focused work by the end of the course. The students were offered the possibility to implement a small additional programming example after the core examples.

5.3.3 Operationalization of Variables

The study considered the following variables to measure learning performance: (1) *Course*: the overall course performance; (2) *P0-P3*: the performance in the four individual assignments of the practical part, which are summarized as *P*; (3) *Exam*: the performance in the theoretical exam. Furthermore the study considered three variables measuring the blogging activity of and within the community of the authors: (1) *Posts*: the number of postings by an author; (2) *Bloggers:* the number of active bloggers in the community of the author; (3) *All-Activity:* the number of overall posts in the community of the author. Figure 5-1 depicts the context of these variables and the previously defined hypotheses.

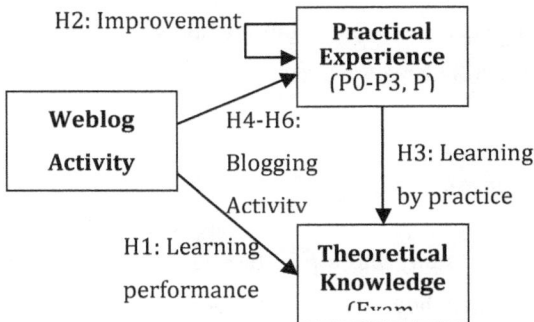

Figure 5-1: Operationalization of Variables

5.3.4 Technical Setup

The students were offered the possibility to use a modified version of the ELGG software[42] to create and maintain e-Portfolios, as depicted in Figure 5-2. The focus in

---

[42] http://elgg.org/, accessed 2008-05-19

the course of this experiment was the usage of the weblog functionality, although ELGG offers additional possibilities. In order to deal with privacy concerns of the participants, the posts within the blog could either be made accessible to everybody or registered members of the university only, at the discretion of the students.

The participating students were organized in individual communities of learning, one for each mentoring tutor. These communities offered a central point to read the weblogs of each member. Moreover, they provided the possibility to subscribe to all posts of the community's members via a single RSS feed. The mentoring tutors themselves committed posts to the community regularly in order to encourage the students to participate. The contents posted by the individual communities where highly different from each other, but quite coherent within the communities. While one of the communities focused on giving help on setting up and utilizing various Integrated Development Environments (IDEs), the second community was leading a meta discussion on the lecture. The third and fourth group were mostly concerned with language-specific postings about C++. Finally, the fifth group had evolved to a private discussion between two community members with almost no postings from other members. Figure 5-3 displays a tag cloud summarizing the topics of one of these groups.

5.3.5 Post-study Survey

The final part of the case study was a post-test questionnaire. On the one hand, this was intended to investigate how the level of experience with social media in general and weblogs through the course of this lecture has changed within the 10 months since the pre-test questionnaire. On the other hand, the effects of the blogging on learning habits were of interest. Unfortunately, only 67 participants completed the survey, which were 12.9% of the participants. Twenty of these had kept a weblog during the lecture.

Figure 5-2: Screenshot of the modified ELGG environment

Figure 5-3: Tag cloud of sample tutorial community

As far as the comparison to the results of the pre-test survey is concerned, the general part of the survey showed a similar result as far as the demographic details, communication channels used and IT infrastructure is concerned. Only 5.9% of the participants had not heard about weblogs in the post-study survey. 61.2% of the participants had used weblogs as readers. The 20 students who had used the weblogs during the lecture classified it either as *active use as author* (31.7%), *for learning* (21.1%), or *guided use in lectures* (47.2%).

As far as the feedback on the use of weblogs during the lecture is concerned, 21% of the blogging students felt a positive effect on their learning performance in the practical part of the lecture. 11% perceived a positive effect on the performance in the theoretical exam. 35% stated that they enjoyed keeping the weblogs.

67% of the students stated that they had read other participants' weblogs during the lecture. 44% of these participants stated that they benefitted from reading these weblogs in the practical part of the lecture. 21% stated that they benefited in the theoretical exam.

5.4 Analysis and Results

The focus of the study was to verify whether the use of weblogs on a voluntary basis would influence the learning performance in a programming lecture. Thus, significant relations between the use of weblogs and the performance in the lecture were sought based on the comparison of a test and a comparison group.

5.4.1 Basic Statistics

As previously stated the total number of participants was 517. 246 of these students formed the test group. The remaining 271 students formed the comparison group. 66 students (27%) of the test group chose to keep a weblog during the course.

The number of individual posts varied from one post to 23 posts during the test period. The mean number of postings for the blogging participants is 3.8 and the standard deviation is 3.82.

5.4.2 Course Performance and Continual Improvement (H1, H2)

In order to determine a possible relationship of the authoring of weblogs with the overall course performance the Pearson's correlation coefficient was calculated for the overall course performance and the activity of the individual students based on the two groups. For the test group the activity was defined as the act of writing a weblog, while for the comparison group this was defined as the act of submitting the additional assignment. The level of activity was defined as the number of postings and the extent of the additional assignment respectively. The analysis yielded a significant correlation both for the test group and the comparison group in both cases. As the weblogs were voluntary for the test group and could be replaced with an additional example, the activity for any of these two options is analyzed for the test group additionally. The results are summarized in Table 5-2.

Table 5-2. Correlation of activity and course performance

	Active	Level	Any[43]
Test Group	0.369*	0.252*	0.383*
Comparison Group	0.523*	0.468*	

*.   Correlation is significant at the 0.01 level

According to these results, the activity of the student in the additional parts of the lecture (weblog or additional example) is related to the overall course performance, a relation that was likely. Anyway, the fact of submitting additional examples is correlated stronger than the fact of keeping a weblog, and even keeping a weblog or submitting the additional example. Thus, H1 cannot be confirmed.

---

[43] Activity either with weblogs or additional example

Subsequently the relation of the previously defined activities on the improvement from one assignment to the other was investigated. As shown in Table 5-3 no significant correlation could be found for the fact of keeping a weblog and the improvement during the assignments. There is a significant correlation as far as the number of postings is concerned, but the corresponding correlation for the comparison group is almost identical, so H2 could not be affirmed.

Table 5-3. Correlation of activity and continuous improvement

	Active	Level
Test Group	0.100	0.171*
Comparison Group	0.219*	0.173*

*.   Correlation is significant at the 0.01 level

5.4.3 Learning from Practical Examples (H3)

A first analysis of the two variables *Exam* and *P* yields a high correlation of 0.884 for the test group and 0.812 for the comparison group, which both are significant at the 0.01 level. Obviously there is a relation between the practical performance and the success in the theoretical exam, and this relation is stronger in the case of the test group.

Subsequently a regression analysis was conducted to investigate the influence of the fact of keeping a weblog as well as the activity within this blog on the ratio of success in the exam by success in the practical part. The results are depicted in Table 5-4.

Both variables are significant predictors of the success ratio of theoretical exam by practical part of the lecture. In other words, students who keep a weblog are better at transferring a good result in the practical part of the lecture into the performance at the theoretical exam. H3 can be confirmed.

Table 5-4. Predictive values for activity

Dependent variable / Predictor	Exam/P	
	R	P-value
Activity	0.113**	6.39E-08
Level	0.025*	0.014

*. Correlation is significant at the 0.05 level
**. Correlation is significant at the 0.01 level

5.4.4 Practical Performance (H4, H5, H6)

A series of regression analyses was conducted to determine the relationship of weblog writing activity within a community on the learning performance in the practical part of the lecture. These communities were formed from the students of each of the five tutors coaching the test group. The results are summarized in Table 5-5.

Table 5-5. Predictive values of Posts, Bloggers and Activity

Dependent variable / Predictor	P	
	R	P-value
Posts	0.089**	1.89E-06
Bloggers	0.025*	0.012
All-Activity	0.105**	1.92E-07

*. Correlation is significant at the 0.05 level
**. Correlation is significant at the 0.01 levels

As shown above, the variables *Posts, Bloggers,* and *All-Activity* are significant predictors of the performance in the practical part of the lecture. In other words, students who blog more often generally performed better in the practical part of the lecture. Moreover, communities with a higher number of bloggers perform better overall and finally communities with a higher overall activity in the weblogs perform better. H4, H5 and H6 can be affirmed.

5.5 Discussion

On the one hand, several of the previously defined hypotheses have been confirmed by the study. The activity in weblogs can be used as a predictor for the learning performance within a programming lecture. On the other hand, two of these hypotheses could not be confirmed. General statements about a superior impact of continuous engagement by blogging as compared to focused engagement by the end of a lecture cannot be affirmed.

Impact on individual performance. As far as individuals are concerned, their own activity within a lecture accompanying weblog can be a predictor for the learning performance in the practical part of this lecture. Students, who engage in the process of posting about their concurrent work, become more active in the reflection on their work and are able to improve their practical work. Moreover, blogging students are better at transferring a good performance in the practical part of the lecture into theoretical knowledge.

Impact on the community. As far as the communities of students are concerned, both the number of bloggers and the number of posts can be used as a predictor for the overall performance in this community. There is an improvement for the whole of the community in communities with a high number of bloggers, respectively a high activity in the weblogs.

5.6 Limitations

The presented study suffers from three limitations. Firstly, the participants of the survey were limited to one location, the Graz University of Technology. Subsequent related studies at other universities would improve the validity of the results.

Secondly, the study was designed to be as unobtrusive to the normal flow of the lecture as possible. Therefore, the pre- and post-test questionnaires were implemented as voluntary online questionnaires, which were completed only by a fraction of the participants. Thus, the relation to the empiric part is limited.

Finally, those students in the test group who chose not to keep a weblog were provided with the same alternative as the comparison group. This approach was chosen due to the same reasons as for the second limitation, though it restricts the influence of weblog activity on the outcome.

5.7 Summary and Conclusions

Based on overall popularity of weblogs and theories of constructivist learning, the approach to use weblogs as learning logs has been used in individual situations for some time, though the overall adoption rate is still quite low, in general society as well as in education. As far as the education in programming languages is concerned, weblogs seem especially well suited due to the impact on reflection of the own work and thus continuous engagement with the learning content.

The activity in such weblogs seems well suited as a predictor for the performance in such practical parts of a programming lecture. They are used to express current experiences during the programming tasks, problems, hints for the setup of the programming environment, and last but not least the reflection of the own performance.

The low rate of 30% of the students who engaged in the blogging activity, and the results of the pre- and post-study surveys hint on a relatively low knowledge and level of experience with weblogs. Therefore, there is still an improved need for instructors to incorporate weblogs in their courses.

Chapter 6 Learning from the Others – Peer Review in the Community

Peer review is a well-known tool to encourage students to engage more deeply with a subject. In the era of "wisdom of the crowds", a collaborative approach to review and improve the deliverables of software development lectures offers a contemporary supplement to the learning process. This chapter reports on the implementation of a peer review tool designed to support students in a basic programming lecture. It covers the integration of tutor and peer feedback and the incorporation of the results into the grading of the students.

6.1 Peer Review in Higher Education

Reviewing and assessing programming examples is a strenuous and time-consuming task for any lecturer, especially if the goal is the provision of extended feedback to the students. This is especially true for courses with a high number of students. Automatic grading of such examples by functional tests gives only dissatisfying results in this context, as the functionality of a submitted example is only part of the assessment criteria. Other important aspects are the applied approach, the elegancy of the implementation, and the coding standard. As such, automatic testing environments are not suitable to assist in this task.

One possible approach is to outsource certain steps to humans, as proposed in human computation [Kosorukoff, 2001], and divide the task onto multiple individuals. A similar approach is used in academic publications. Here, peer review has been used as an instrument for assessment and quality control for a long time.

In the context of learning, peer review describes the process of students reviewing the work of their fellow students. In the case of integration into the formal grading process, it may also be labeled peer assessment. Despite the fact that peer review in this context offers a possibility to provide more and better feedback to the individual students receiving the review, it also improves the learning process for students giving the review, due to the deeper occupation with the subject and the possibility to potentially see various approaches.

6.2 Related Work

The positive effect of peer review on the learning process has been highlighted by several researchers, as it is considered to be effective in promoting higher cognitive skills [Fallows and Chandramohan, 2001]. Moreover, in certain contexts like programming lectures it depicts real-world practices in industry [Sullivan, 1994].

A web based peer assessment tool has been developed at the University of Warwick, which allows anonymous peer assessment. The assessment involves possible group discussion within one grading group and takes the quality of the program and the quality of the marking into account. The marking of the examples is based on a fixed set of criteria. The assessing student may choose the extent to which the criterion is met. [Sitthiworachart and Joy, 2004b; Sitthiworachart and Joy, 2004a]

Another approach developed at the North Carolina State University is concerned with the peer grading of Web pages in Computer Science courses. There is a direct, yet double blind communication between reviewers and authors via a shared Web page. Like in the previously presented approach, the quality of the feedback is graded by the original author. [Gehringer, 2001]

One further possibility is to focus the review on the coding standard, implementing a code review process (CRP). This approach is based on the previously mentioned common practice in academic publishing as well as on the industry practice to enforce coding standards. A case study showed that not only did the students' performance in learning coding standards improve, but also the communication between the students and the critical engagement with other aspects of the assignment was fostered. [Xiaosong, 2006]

The focus of another approach developed at the University of Oklahoma is on the team aspect, designing the exercises especially to give teamwork experience. Original student work or work altered by the instructor is first reviewed individually, providing a fixed set of questions to be answered. The results are subsequently discussed in class. [Trytten, 2005]

A key criterion in the context of peer review is the quality of the feedback. This is also a major concern about peer review in academic peer review [McMartin et al., 2004]. In this context, the lack of feedback in certain review fields is one of the main problems, which can also be mapped on the learning application of peer review.

Objectivity is another criterion to the quality of feedback. Subsequently fostering the ability of the students for differentiation between objective criteria and personal stands is one of the main issues in designing a peer review process. A possible design principle to achieve this is not to grade students on the content of the reviews received but only on the quality of the reviews given. [Kali and Ronen, 2005]

Another approach at the University of Freiburg focuses on the fact that peer review can be perceived as a specialized form of collaborative learning. In this context, collaboration scripts are used and the integration of screen-recorded presentation is enabled. [Trahasch, 2004]

Finally, peer review may also be used in-class in a lightweight preliminary variant. A quick classification in the four dimensions of correctness, comprehension, worthiness for discussion and similarity to the own solution offers the possibility to identify a subset of student solutions that warrant immediate discussion. [Denning et al., 2007]

6.3 Peer Reviewing Programming Examples

In order to incorporate peer reviews into the learning process of our beginners programming lecture for roughly 500 students we decided to design a peer review system, which allows the annotation of code examples handed in by the students. After individual engagement with example programs, the students are encouraged to engage in collaborative discussion and annotation of a selection of reviewed example programs.

6.3.1 Review Process

Each student receives a randomly composed set of examples with the task to find errors and comment on the quality of the examples. Figure 6-1 shows the design peer review application for the students.

In this application, students add individual remarks to a code example. For each remark, the students may choose from a set of error types. Possible error types include:

- General Comment
- Coding Standard Mistake
- Semantic Error
- Syntactic Error

The remarks can be annotated with a comment. These comments may be assigned to a single line. Alternatively, they can be assigned to multiple adjacent lines (a block) or to non- adjacent lines.

The displayed code is adapted by highlighting language constructs to improve readability. The individual remarks are highlighted using the background-color of the line of code. This presentation is color coded according to the type of error type.

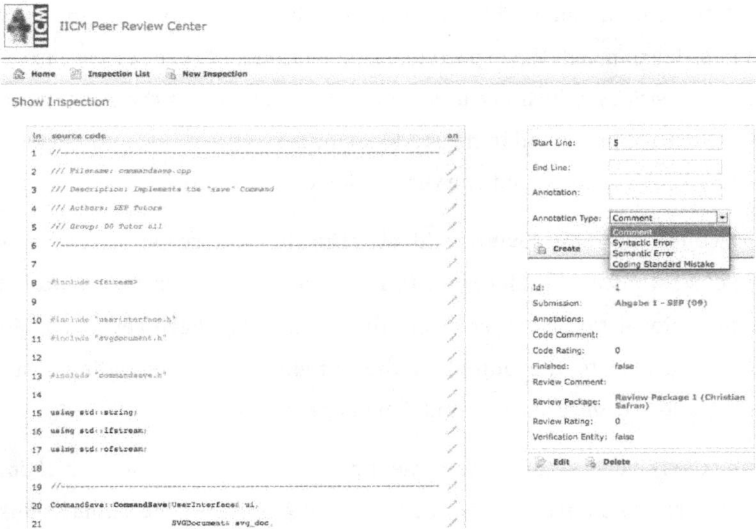

Figure 6-1: Student interface for code comments

6.3.2 Incorporation into Grading

One of our main concerns in the context of peer review was the integration into the lecture grades. In order to encourage a useful feedback process it was aimed to reward both the quality of the original submission as well as the quality of the feedback. To that end both the results of the review and the perceived quality of the review are incorporated into the grading, as proposed in [Sitthiworachart and Joy, 2004b].

Two situations could be malevolent in this context:

⊕ reviewers grade the submissions too positive, ignoring mistakes

⊕ reviewers grade the submissions too negative, marking non-existing mistakes.

To cope with these situations we decided to introduce two verification steps into the review process. Before starting the peer review process, tutors review roughly ten percent of the submissions. This arbitrary number was chosen in our individual situation in order to match the expected tutors' workload. These reviews are the basis for *verification entities*, which are used to check the quality of the peer review. Each assessment package presented to the students for review contains four review entities (non-reviewed submissions) and one verification entity.

The interface for the tutor review is identical to the peer review interface with the difference of a list displaying all review tasks queued for that particular tutor. This list also contains information whether or not the example has been reviewed. Moreover, the tutor has access to the output of the automatic tests, including test results, compiler log, and the log of the valgrind[44] memcheck tool.

Firstly, only the reviews of those assessment packages for which the verification entity was correctly reviewed are incorporated into the grading of the submissions. Other feedback is forwarded to the reviewed student but not considered for grading purposes.

Secondly, the verification entities are again taken into accounting the rating of the review. As it can generally be assumed that the tutors' reviews are at least in some way helpful, only those ratings are incorporated into the grading, which rate the verification entities as medium helpful or better.

In the specific case of our programming lecture we decided to allocate 50% of the assignment's total points to the functional tests, 25% to the results of the peer review and 25% to the rating of the student's own review.

6.3.3 Collaborative Work

After the completion of the review process, the results should be available for the students for reflection, although the publication of all results would not be useful, due to the sheer number. In order to provide useful material we decided to choose those

---

[44] http://valgrind.org/, accessed 2009-04-22

three reviewed submissions with most comments to provide examples of possible improvement. These are complemented by the submissions of those three reviewers, which received the best rating as examples of good work.

As we have already had promising results with the use of a wiki in the process of discussing examination examples, we have decided to use the same platform for the collaborative discussion of these examples from the practical part of our lectures.

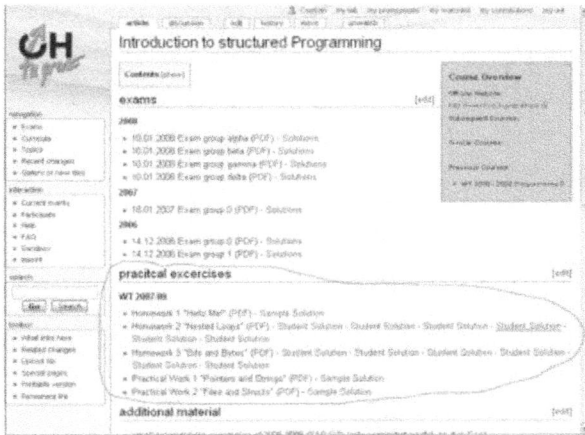

Figure 6-2: Wiki for the support of exam preparation

On this platform, students and lecturers of various courses have the possibility to add information about exams and edit the documents providing material to prepare for exams. This brings the advantage for the students that they are already familiar with the environment the example solutions are published in. Figure 6-2 depicts the wiki page for the programming lecture with the practical example part marked.

6.4 Workflow Summary

Summarizing the sequence of events, the workflow of the peer review application starts with the review of a small amount of the original submission by a tutor. Subsequently students have the possibility to review assessment packages containing review entities and verification entities. Grading only occurs if the level of trust in the review process is assured due to the review of the verification entity. As a next step, the original authors assess the quality of the review. Finally, a selected subset of reviewed submissions is published in a collaborative environment for further discussion. Figure 6-3 summarizes this workflow of the peer review process.

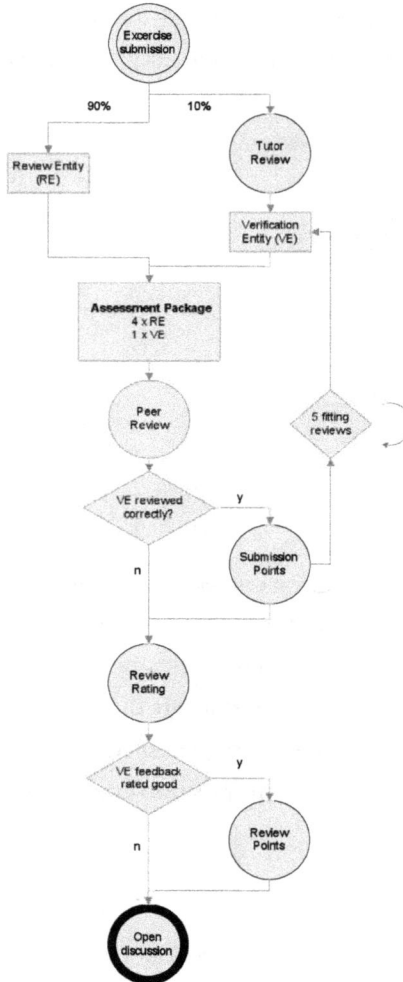

Figure 6-3: Review workflow

6.5 Evaluation

An evaluation of the application of PRC in a beginners' programming lecture was conducted in summer term 2009 and consisted of three areas. First of all a set of correlations of individual aspects of the peer review and the standard assessment of the programming examples by a teacher was analyzed. Secondly, the possible application of peer review as peer assessment to complement standard assessment parts in the lecture was evaluated. Thirdly, the subjective benefit of peer reviewing programs for the participating students was to be investigated.

The evaluation was conducted with a group of 52 volunteering participants of a large first-year programming lecture in computer science curricula. The group consisted of roughly 83% male participants and 17% female participants, matching the student distribution within the curricula involved.

6.5.1 Evaluation Setup

The evaluation was set up to consist of three parts. In a first step, the participants were asked to answer a set of questions regarding their prior knowledge and programming skills in a pre-test survey. In a second step, the participants were asked to solve a short object-oriented programming example matching the topics of the lecture. Subsequently five peers reviewed these pieces of code within 25 minutes, and the results again presented to the authors of the code. The authors were asked to verify the helpfulness of the individual reviews and write a short comment on each of the reviews. Finally, a post-study survey was conducted to evaluate the participants' feelings about the setting applied as well as peer review in general.

6.5.2 Pre-study Survey

In the pre-study survey, the prior knowledge of the participants was investigated. The study consisted of a set of questions regarding the years of practice with programming in general, object-oriented programming, and the programming languages C, C++, C#

and Java. The lectures as well as the programming example in the evaluation were focused on object-oriented programming in C++. Figure 6-4 depicts the results of this questionnaire. In those two categories most relevant to the peer review (OOP and C++), the participants mostly resemble the lectures target audience of beginners with no or little prior experience.

6.5.3 Analysis and Results

The analysis of the evaluation result consists of three parts: the analysis correlation of comments and performance, the evaluation coherence of professional and peer assessment, and the inspection of the participants' impressions.

6.5.3.1 Peers' Comments and Performance

In a first step, the correlation of the quantity of annotation is relayed to the quality of the code and the review. To that end, two terms require definition in the context of this experiment:

- ⊕ Performance: the quality level of one piece of code determined by professional assessment.

- ⊕ Rating: the quality level of a piece of code determined by peer assessment.

These values were compared to the number of general comments, the number of coding standard (cs) mistakes identified, the number of syntax and semantic errors identified and commented, and the overall number of annotations within the peer reviews.

While there is no statistically significant correlation of general comments to one of the two types of quality measurement, there is a statistically significant negative correlation of the number of coding standard mistakes and both measurements. This means that, to a certain level, this number can be used as a predictor for the code quality.

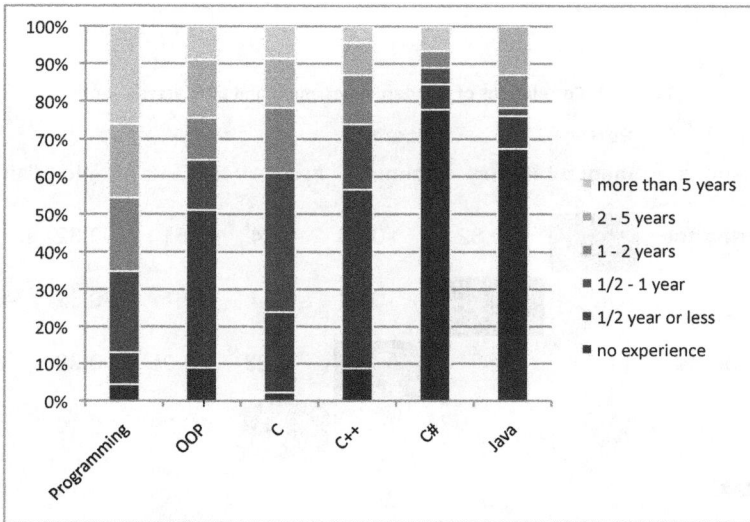

Figure 6-4: Participants prior programming experience

The same is true to an even greater extend, and statistically highly significant, for the number of syntax errors identified. As far as semantic errors are concerned, no statistically significant correlation could be found. Table 6-1 depicts these correlations in detail.

6.5.3.2 Peer Assessment opposed to Standard Assessment

In order to evaluate the possible application to use peer assessment as part of the general assessment of a programming lecture, the individual examples reviewed by the peers have additionally been professionally reviewed by the teacher as a part of the standard assessment of the lecture. A different grading scale was used by the peers and the teachers to reflect the different levels of experience. The peers were asked to rate the programming examples they reviewed with a rating between one (mostly erroneous or wrong) to four (no mistakes and a good solution). The teacher rated the programming examples with 0 to 10 possible points. Both ratings were normalized for the subsequent analyses.

Table 6-1: Correlations of standard assessment and peer assessment

Correlations	Performance	Rating	#comments	#cs	#syntax	#semantic	#all
Performance		0.82**	-0.05	-0.34*	-0.51**	-0.32	-0.51**
Rating			-0.04	-0.34*	-0.67**	-0.32	-0.57**
#comments				-0.23	0.05	-0.28	0.61**
#cs					0.29	0.10	0.34*
#syntax						0.16	0.64**
#semantic							0.29
#all							

*: significant at the 0.05 level

**: significant at the 0.01 level

Table 6-1 depicts, beside the correlation of annotations to quality, also the correlation of professional assessment (performance) and peer assessment (rating). This correlation is 0.82, which is statistically highly significant.

In a first deeper analysis, the individual ratings of the peers were compared to the performance based on the teacher's assessment, deliberately not taking into account the fact that each piece of code has been reviewed several times. Figure 6-5 depicts the results of this comparison. Obviously several peer reviews diverge by a large amount from the performance. The quality of the peer review in relation to the performance was determined by calculating the mean absolute error (MAE) of the peer reviews. In the scenario of individual reviews, the MAE turned out to be 17.03%.

In a second step, the concept of review packages was expanded to the peer assessment by summarizing all ratings of the same piece of code to a mean rating. Figure 6-6 depicts the results of this comparison. The mean ratings are closer to the performance as compared to individual ratings, which also reflects in the MAE, which is 10.3%.

6.5.3.3 Students' opinion on peer review

In a post-study survey, the participants were asked to state their opinion on peer review and peer assessment in the context of beginners programming lectures. The participants were presented a set of seven statements and asked to agree or disagree on a five-value scale. These statements were:

- ⊕ "I was given enough time to do my review."

- ⊕ "Reviewing other participants' code offered a possibility to engage deeper with the topic"

- ⊕ "Reviewing other participants' code provided me with new insights as how to possible solve the problem"

- ⊕ "It was hard to review the other participants code fair (on a social level)"

- ⊕ "It was hard to review the other participants code right (on a competence level)"

- ⊕ "I appreciate the possibility to rate my peers' code in addition to the annotation"

- ⊕ "I appreciate to see the rating my peers gave on my piece of code"

As far as the amount of time for the peer review is concerned, the majority of the participants were content with 25 minutes for five reviews of approximately one page of code. They also agreed widely on the fact that the peer review offered them a possibility to engage deeper with the original task of the programming example. To a lesser extent, the participants agreed that the review offered them new perspectives on alternatively possible solutions.

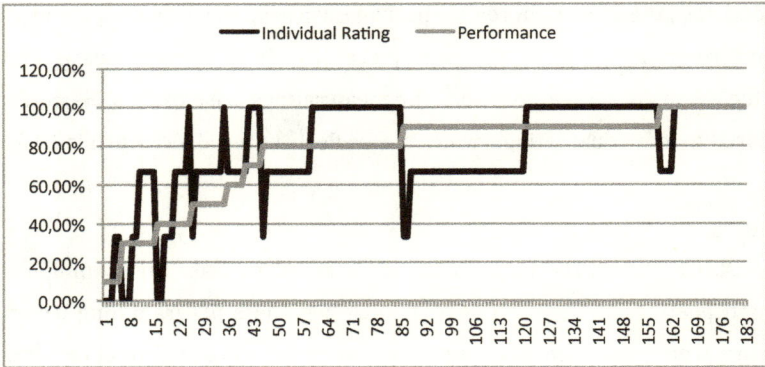

Figure 6-5: Standard assessment vs. peer assessment using individual reviews

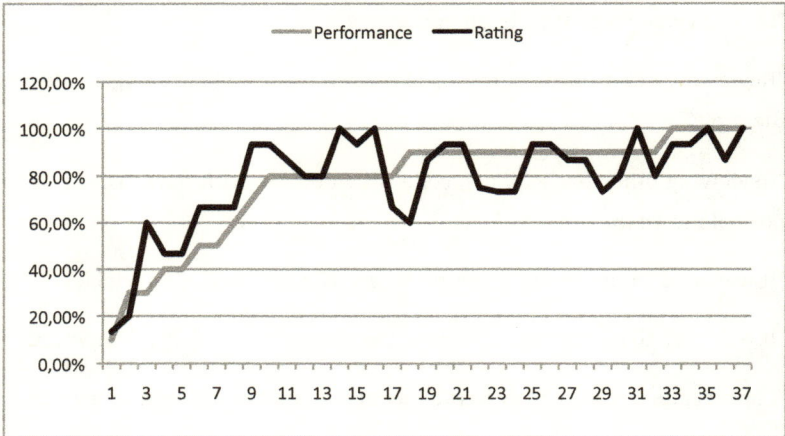

Figure 6-6: Standard assessment vs. peer assessment using review packages

Only a minority of the students agreed that reviewing their peers was hard either on a social or competence level. Surprisingly only a minority appreciated the possibility to rate their peers in addition to the annotation of the code or even to see their peers' ratings of their own code. Figure 6-7 depicts the results of the post-study survey in detail.

As far as the general feedback on the peers' annotations is concerned, most students were positive about the usefulness of at least some of the comments. The most interesting answers in this context were:

- „Very nice and very helpful comments"

- „Some mistakes were falsely identified, although generally ok"

- „I have nor been reminded of obvious mistakes"

- „Very interesting method to analyze code"

- „Helpful as it is written by other students, and I understand them better"

- „Several very useful comments, but also one totally senseless one"

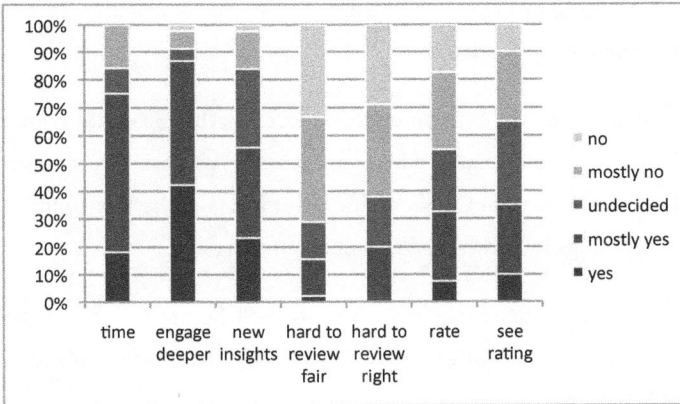

Figure 6-7: Results of the post-study survey

Finally, the participants were asked to decide for each individual review they received, whether it was helpful feedback or not. 10.8% of the participants replied that none of the reviews was helpful. The remaining participants found at least one of the reviews helpful, for 18.92% even all of the reviews were useful feedback.

6.6 Summary and Outlook

We have presented a peer review approach for the context of a beginners' programming language course. It is based on the concept of code annotation and focuses on the improvement of the quality of the produced code as well as on the improvement of the quality of the review. A further central part is the comparison to tutor reviews in order to gain a level of trust in the student review. The output of the peer review process is published in a wiki to allow further collaborative engagement with the topic.

Furthermore, we have presented the evaluation of an online peer review solution in the context of university computer science curricula, based on the notion of code annotation. The review aspect of the application was in general well received by the participants of this evaluation and lead to the expected result of deeper engagement with the programming example. The vast majority of participants received at least some helpful comments as feedback.

As far as the integration into assessment is concerned, the mean assessment over five reviews yielded acceptable results when compared to professional assessment of the same pieces of code. Yet, from the students' point of view, the possibility to rate their peers or see the ratings they received was not so important.

Based on the results of this evaluation the PRC will be applied to our future years' programming lectures to offer additional peer feedback on the beginning programming examples.

Chapter 7 Applying Collaborative Mind Maps for Learning

Among the various methodologies to support cognitive processes and enhance the transfer and acquisition of knowledge, mapping methodologies are among the best known approaches. A *map* is a (2-dimensional) structured visualization of knowledge. Perhaps the widest known approach is the application of a *mind map*, although it is often falsely used for a broad range mapping methodologies. In fact, the term only identifies one of the numerous possible visualizations.

7.1 Introduction

The various types of *maps* are strongly tied to learning and teaching. As far as learning is concerned, they provide a tool to support cognitive processes. As far as teaching is concerned, they are useful to support the transfer of knowledge. Moreover, they can be used in assessment to validate prior knowledge and evaluate learning performance. All of these applications are bound to the concept that cognitive processes can be enhanced, if they are exteriorized and visualized [Jonassen, 2001].

Mind maps are one such mapping methodology introduced by Tony Buzan in 1970. It is focused on the stimulation of the whole brain in creative processes [Buzan, 1976]. A mind map is a hierarchical two-dimensional structure with a central topic. *Ideas* are arranged around this subject as annotated branches. These branches may fork further into subordinate ideas. Another key characteristic of mind maps is the fact that the relation between the individual ideas is not labeled.

Mind mapping is considered efficient due to five characteristics. Mind maps are keyword oriented, which represent concepts related to the central topic. They have loose syntax and semantics, resulting in association being the only relation between the key words. Due to these two facts, mind maps are fast and easily developed. They provide a high level overview, as the mind map can be viewed as a whole. Finally, mind maps are evocative. Due to the use of both brain hemispheres, the mind maps evoke the context of the situation later on.

Scenarios for application to learning and teaching are bound to the concept that cognitive processes can be enhanced, if they are exteriorized and visualized [Jonassen, 2001]. Several such applications have been presented over the years (see below), but the technological and social development of the recent years offers new possibilities to bring mind maps into the context of social software and apply such tools in education.

This chapter presents one such social Web tool for collaborative online mind mapping designed for application in higher education. Subsequently scenarios for the application of such a tool for learning, teaching, and assessing are discussed.

7.2 Related Work

Mind maps can be best used to present knowledge structured around a single, core concept, due to the treelike structure applied. In case of the visualization of a larger body of knowledge, as in a knowledge repository, mind maps provide only insufficient support. Concept maps, a visualization technology based on a graph of equal-ranked concepts as nodes, and labelled relations as edges, have been identified as better suitable. [Weideman and Kritzinger, 2003]

In comparison to several alternative technologies used for the visualization of knowledge, such as concept maps, or conceptual diagrams, the general usefulness of mind maps in the organization of content has been proved. Yet, a combination with the other techniques has been shown to be most useful, as far as collaborative work is concerned. The application to this context is mainly focused on providing an overview and organizing content. [Eppler, 2006]

In the context of education, mind mapping can be used in various analysis processes. The application to case analysis and group process analysis in executive information has been shown as possible and useful. Students accept the technique as easy and self-explanatory. [Mento et al., 1999]

As far as efficacy of mind mapping is concerned, an evaluation in comparison to self-selected study yielded positive results for the mind mapping approach. In this evaluation, students were asked to read a 600-word passage and study the content without prior knowledge. Those students requested to use mind maps for learning showed a 10% increase in the accuracy of their recall of the passage. [Farrand et al., 2002]

Another application area in education is computer science curricula. The semi-structured approach of mind maps can enhance the early phase of object-oriented design. In this phase of problem exploration, mind maps have been shown to be a suitable tool to assist students. [Martin, 2007]

Furthermore, mind maps can be applied as active learning tools. In this context, they are applied to enhance critical thinking and problem-solving skills. Learning modules should be designed in three phases, following the "think-rap-map" approach. In a first phase, the students develop individual preliminary maps. These are peer reviewed and collaboratively discussed in the second phase. The third phase is used to create a final integrative map [Willis and Miertschin, 2006]. As far as technology is concerned, tablet PCs provide a suitable technological base for the application of mind maps in this context[Willis and Miertschin, 2005].

7.3 Development of a Collaborative Mind-Mapping Tool

In order to provide a tool that supports collaborative work on mind maps in learning and education, a list of prerequisites was defined. In a basic step, general requirements for mind mapping tools can be defined based on Buzan's recommendations in the original mind mapping book [Buzan and Buzan, 2006].

Emphasis should be used in order to highlight individual parts of the mind map. This includes the application of different colors as well as the use of images throughout the mind map. The importance of individual nodes can be emphasized by variation of the font size. Finally, in order to enhance the map later on, spacing should be organized and appropriate. As far as computer-based mind mapping tools are concerned, this includes the possibility of freely adding and moving nodes.

Association is the second technique recommended by Buzan. Individual node can be brought into context by adding arrows. Moreover, colors can also be used to create association, as well as using certain icons as codes.

Finally, **clearness** denotes the goal to make the mind map understandable at the first glance. This includes using only one keyword per node. All keywords should be printed. The map should be drawn on blank paper. Lines should match the length of the keywords.

Aside from the basic requirements, any mind mapping tool should meet a set of additional requirements. These requirements were identified for collaborative mind-mapping tools intended for technology-enhanced learning. These requirements were formulated after a series of interviews with lecturers at Graz University of Technology.

Firstly, such an application must provide the possibility to **attach** additional information to the individual nodes of the map. These attachments can be documents as well as links. Moreover it is proposed to add links to external knowledge bases and search engines querying for the node's text, as proposed for the approach of the digital background library [Safran et al., 2006]. Such links can be links to Wikipedia, Google, del.icio.us, and similar services.

Secondly, a detailed **history** of user actions must be stored. On the one hand, this history can be used for the rollback of user interaction. On the other hand, it provides a valuable tool in collaborative work to visualize the contributions of the individual participants.

Furthermore, collaborative work on the same mind map must be possible in a **remote setting**. In this setting, the participants work on a distributed set of computers, either synchronously or asynchronously.

A further collaborative mode is the work in a **local setting**. In this setting, multiple users work on the same computer on the same mind map. A collaborative mind-mapping tool should be enhanced by the possibility to switch between active users in a local setting, in order to retain a correct history for the individual users. A traceable, comprehensive design of the mind map can be useful for participants joining the collaborating team later on.

Moreover, a collaborative mind-mapping tool for technology-enhanced learning should provide a feature to **fork** an existing mind map in order to allow separate work on individual parts.

Finally, the tool must provide a feature to **merge** existing mind maps. This is necessary to continue collaborative work on forked mind maps, but can also be used to create a united mind map of two independently created maps.

Based on these requirements the most popular mind mapping tools, Mind Manager[45] and Freemind[46], have been evaluated [Safran et al., 2006]. In a first step a heuristic evaluation based on the Nielsen heuristics [Nielsen and Mack, 1994] has been conducted. Although all tools provide a sufficiently well designed user experience concerning the basic requirements for mind mapping, the additional requirements were fulfilled by none of the evaluated tools.

In order to meet the additional requirements described above, a collaborative, Web-based mind mapping tool has been developed [Strouhal, 2009]. Figure 7-1 depicts a screenshot of a mind map created with this collaborative tool.

---

[45] http://www.mindjet.com, accessed 2009-09-10

[46] http://freemind.sourceforge.net, accessed 2009-09-10

The collaborative mind mapping tool is based on the notion of creating mind maps and sharing them for individual other users or the public to start collaborative work. Each mind map is based on a central topic. Nodes can be added to the central topic or other nodes. These nodes can be freely placed and moved. For each node, file attachments and images can be uploaded. The images are automatically rescaled to fit into the mind map. Furthermore, links and icons can be added to the node.

As an additional service, formatted notes can be written with a WYSIWYG[47] editor and attached to the nodes. Moreover, a primitive task management system is implemented to define task states, start and due dates, as well as task priorities to individual nodes.

Finally, the collaborative mind-mapping tool offers a service to propose suiting concepts as sub nodes. The list of possible concepts is derived from other publically accessible maps sharing a nod with the same keyword. Another feature for the proposing of node keywords is a synonym tool proposing related keywords.

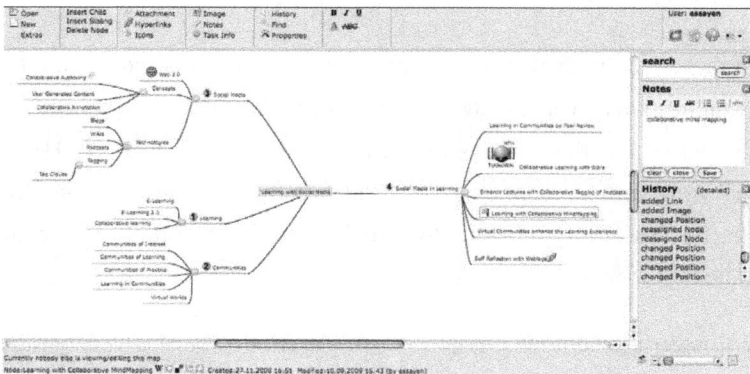

Figure 7-1: Screenshot of the collaborative mind-mapping tool

---

[47] What you see is what you get

Collaborative work is possible in a remote and a local setting. For the remote setting, changes done by other users are polled from the server in a predefined interval. The mind-mapping tool provides a basic messaging system to communicate with other users collaborating on the same map. For local collaboration, a fast user switch is implemented. Figure 7-2 depicts the user switch dialog.

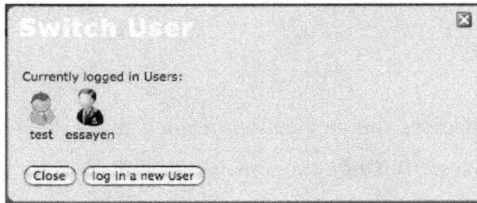

Figure 7-2: Fast user switch dialog

In comparison to existing offline solutions like Mind Manager or Freemind, this tool offers the advantage of access via a Web browser instead of the installation of software. Moreover, these tools provide only rudimentary support of collaborative work. However, our tool requires an online connection. Online tools like Mind Meister[48] provide collaborative features, but lack features to track the individual participation of the collaborating users.

7.4 Application Scenarios

The collaborative mind mapping tool described above was developed to support technology-enhanced learning in higher education context. Beside the general requirements described above, a set of possible application scenarios in the context of a university software development course have been defined. These scenarios serve

---

[48] http://www.mindmeister.com, accessed 2009-09-10

both as a source for additional requirements, as well a possibilities to evaluate the usefulness of the collaborative mind mapping approach. Although the scenarios where evaluated with our own collaborative mind mapping tool, they are basically suitable for every mind mapping tool applicable for collaborative work, although the enhanced feature like local collaborative work and the user-linked history provide additional value for educators.

7.4.1 Mind Maps for Software Development Education – User Requirements

The first scenario addresses the application of mind maps in the context of practical programming exercises. During the analysis and design phase of software development, UML[49] is used for visualization. However, as UML is used for modeling and thus is a structured approach, it restricts also restricts possibilities in visualization. Applying mind maps to gather user stories and explore the user wish has thus been proposed as a semi-structured intermediate level in software development [Hiranabe, 2007]. In this approach, a mind map is used to capture this user wish. Later on, this mind map is converted into UML use case diagrams.

Beyond the application to general software development, this approach offers a tool for the education of beginners in software development. These students are usually not competent in the modeling of use cases with UML. Using mind maps to gather the user wish provides a semi-structured intermediate step to the actual modeling process.

The scenario is set in a first-year computer science lecture addressing software engineering. The task is to teach the basic programming skills and bring the students, who often have varying levels of experience, to a same basic level. In this

---

[49] Unified Modelling Language

heterogeneous environment collaborative mind mapping is proposed to solve communication difficulties among these students.

After the lecturer has handed out the original exercise instruction, the students are requested to collaboratively create a mind map depicting the *user wish* described with this document. This mind map is later on used to be converted into a use case diagram or serves directly as basis for the software design process.

This scenario has been evaluated with a group of seven students, split into teams of two and three. The two double teams were asked to collaborate remotely with the mind-mapping tool, while the team of three was asked to collaborate locally. Subsequently, the students were interviewed and asked to fill out a survey. The survey consisted of a series of statements, which could be rated in a five-point scale from total agreement to total disagreement.

When asked for the feasibility of relaying the exercise instruction into a mind map, the students stated that it was easy or very easy. The mind map moreover was perceived as giving a good overview of the exercise. Table 7-1 provides the detailed results for these questions.

Table 7-1: Creation of the mind map

	Converting the instructions was easy.	The mind map provided a bad overview.
Agree totally	28.57 %	14.29 %
Agree	71.43 %	14.29 %
Undetermined	0.00 %	14.29 %
Disagree	0.00 %	57.14 %
Disagree totally	0.00 %	0.00 %

In a second step, the students were asked whether they discovered new connections of the individual parts of the exercise, or had improved their understanding of already connections already known. Although undecided, whether new connections had been discovered, the students stated to have their understanding improved. Table 7-2 provides the details of the student's answers.

Table 7-2: Connections of the individual parts.

	I saw new connections.	I understand connections better.
Agree totally	0.00 %	14.29 %
Agree	28.57 %	28.57 %
Undetermined	42.86 %	42.86 %
Disagree	28.57 %	14.29 %
Disagree totally	0.00 %	0.00 %

Finally the students were asked for their opinion of the suitability of this approach for modeling the user wish, whether or not the creation of the mind map affects their software development process, and whether the mind map was suitable to visualize the exercise instructions.

In the interview, the students stated that they perceived the work with the mind-mapping tool as "rather easy" and "quite comfortable". As alternative techniques for the modeling of the user wish, the students proposed collaborative working with Google Docs, drawing mind maps with pen and paper, and using UML without any intermediate step.

Table 7-3: Review of the suitability for the task.

	Not suitable for user wish.	Affects my development process.	Suitable for instructions
Agree totally	0.00 %	0.00 %	42.86 %
Agree	14.29 %	0.00 %	57.14 %
Undetermined	0.00 %	57.14 %	0.00 %
Disagree	42.86 %	42.86 %	0.00 %
Disagree totally	42.86 %	0.00 %	0.00 %

7.4.2 Mind Maps for Learning

As detailed above, mind mapping has been proposed as a tool to encourage critical thinking and active learning. The application of mind maps as a tool for learning has resulted in improved accuracy of the student's recapitulation of information. In the context of learning the collaborative mind, mapping tool is suggested as a utility for collaborative reflection on a problem or problem domain.

This scenario is likewise set in a beginners' programming lecture, but addresses the preparation for a written exam focused on the theoretical part of software development. Students are encouraged to work in teams and collaboratively generate mind maps visualizing the basic principles of object-oriented programming. This scenario was evaluated with a group of seven students working in two teams. In coherence to the first evaluation, the students were subsequently interviewed and asked to fill out a survey.

Analogously to the first evaluation, the students were first asked for the feasibility of creating a mind map from the lecture and the quality of the overview it gave. Subsequently the students were asked whether the creation of the mind map made them realize new connections of the individual concepts of the theoretic part of the lecture, or if it helped to improve the understanding of connections already known. Table 7-4 gives an overview on the results for these questions.

Table 7-4: Creation of the mind map and connections of concepts

	Easy to convert	Bad overview	New Connections	Known Connections
Agree totally	0.00 %	0.00 %	0.00 %	0.00 %
Agree	71.43 %	28.57 %	14.29 %	42.86 %
Undetermined	28.57 %	0.00 %	71.43 %	57.14 %
Disagree	0.00 %	71.43 %	14.29 %	0.00 %
Disagree totally	0.00 %	0.00 %	0.00 %	0.00 %

In a next step the students were asked whether they considered the creation of the mind map an appropriate preparation for the exam, or whether they would use a pre-created mind map for learning.

Table 7-5: Mind maps as learning material.

	Create a mind map for learning	Use pre-created map
Agree totally	57.14 %	14.29 %
Agree	28.57 %	85.71%
Undetermined	14.29 %	0.00 %
Disagree	0.00 %	0.00 %
Disagree totally	0.00 %	0.00 %

In the interview, the students considered the collaborative mind-mapping tool "helpful" although it was considered as "still having a few bugs". As alternative tools, the students proposed a wiki system or Google Docs.

7.4.3 Mind Mapping for Assessment

The participants in the evaluation of the second scenario proposed the application of mind maps as parts of the assessment process of the lecture. Based on this notion and the "think-rap-map" approach of Willis [Willis and Miertschin, 2005] a third scenario has been developed.

As an addition to other assessment parts, the collaborative creation of mind maps in teams of two is proposed. Each team is assigned a set of two concepts, which serve as central ideas for a mind map. The teams start with individual work. Subsequently, the team partner peer reviews the corresponding other mind map. In a final step, each peer revises his own mind map. The collaborative mind mapping tools provides the features to track the individual peers' work in the final mind map to assess the mapping quality. This scenario will be evaluated in winter term 2009/10.

7.5 Summary and Conclusions

Mind maps are a technique for the visualization of knowledge centered around a central topic. A set of requirements for computer-aided mind mapping tools in the context of technology-enhanced learning has been presented. Based on these requirements a prototype for a Web-based collaborative mind-mapping tool has been developed. Three possible scenarios for the application of such a tool in higher education computer science curricula have finally been presented.

First evaluations have shown that students reacted positively to the mind-mapping tool. The application to the scenarios was likewise considered beneficial. Additional evaluation in an assessment scenario and the development of quantitative measures for all three scenarios is necessary to complete the evaluation of this approach.

Chapter 8 Collaborative Learning with Wikis

Recent years have shown the remarkable potential use of Web 2.0 technologies in education, especially in the context of informal learning. The application of *wikis* to collaborative work is one example of this theory. The support of learning in those fields of education which are strongly based on visual location-based information could also benefit from *geo-tagging*, a technique that has become popular lately, and *m-learning,* which allows learning *in-the-field.* This chapter presents first developments in the combination of these three concepts into a geospatial wiki for higher education, *TUGeowiki.* Our solution proposal supports mobile scenarios where textual data and images are managed and retrieved in the field as well as some desktop scenarios in the context of *collaborative e-learning.* Within this scope, one critical issue arises while adding and updating textual information via the collaborative interface, which can be cumbersome in mobile scenarios. To solve this problem, we integrated another popular concept into our solution approach, *microblogging.* Thus, the information pushed via short messages from mobile clients or microblogging tools to our m-Learning environment enables the creation of *wiki-micropages* as basis for subsequent collaborative learning scenarios.

8.1 Geotagging and Civil Engineering

In subjects such as civil engineering, architecture, geology etc. education is mostly based on visual information. According to Brohn [Brohn, 1983] "the language of intuition is visual, just as the language of analysis is abstract and symbolic". This is especially true in the field of civil engineering where sketches and drawings are highly necessary, because there is a strong relationship between nature and mathematical models [Ebner et al., 2006a]. Learning by studying existing load bearing models is essential for becoming a good engineer.

Furthermore, every building can be seen as a unique object at a precise location. So on-site excursions and field studies are common and are used to give learners more practical examples of what real-life situations look like. One of the most difficult tasks is to find an appropriate physical relationship to describe an engineering model because of the complex coherences. To represent nature with a simple and calculable structure is the first job of a structural engineer.

These arguments particularize the necessity of images, especially in connection with real-world locations, for certain curricula. Nevertheless, not only help images to plan and understand buildings, also geographical information is of interest:

- ⊕ Where is a building located geographically?

- ⊕ Which types of buildings are especially predominant in certain areas?

- ⊕ In the case of large projects (streets, tunnels, hydraulic structures), where are the different contract sections?

There are many more questions, which can be answered by providing global geographical coordinates. From a technical perspective it can be pointed out, that nowadays mobile phones with on-board GPS modules facilitate the addition of coordinates to pictures. Moreover, access to the World Wide Web is readily available with state-of-the art phones, either via mobile or wireless networks.

This chapter addresses the research question on how the learning experience for students of civil engineering or likewise visual- and location-based curricula can be enhanced. The application of geotagged images and texts is proposed in this context. Students, as well as lecturers, should be provided with the possibility of taking geotagged photos in field studies or excursions and upload these to a wiki system in order to collaboratively write articles on the corresponding locations. Appropriate map material should automatically be included to these articles.

8.2 Theoretical Background & Related Work

Today, the organization of learning is changing, especially in secondary schools and universities. However, in this context, new technologies offer an opportunity for pupils and students to communicate and interact with multi-medial learning resources and simulated environments [Holzinger, 2002]. Consequently, technology can enhance motivation, which is a vital aspect of learning [Holzinger, 1997], deliver information when needed, and encourage to *solve problems* and *satisfy curiosity* [Sharples et al., 2002]. Most of all, new technologies also offer the possibility to *scaffold* learners through an extended process of capturing and organizing *situated activities* [Sharples, 2000].

In recent years, use of computers in education has mostly been focused on enhancing learning in formal settings, typically in the traditional classroom or computer lab [Mifsud, 2002]. However, learning does not only take place within such formal learning settings. The use of mobile devices could expand learning possibilities and solve the problem of being tied to a particular location.

Generally, the combination of e-learning and mobile computing is called *mobile learning* (m-learning) and promises the access to applications that support learning anywhere, anytime [Tatar et al., 2003]. Due to technological progress, the efficiency of the hardware is nowadays considered as a solved problem. However, innovative, affordable and usable software remains the greatest challenge. For example [Norris and Soloway, 2004] argue that handhelds should support project-based learning in context, that is, using the mobile phone as an integral part of a learning activity.

In m-learning the issue of technology acceptance has been largely overlooked although previous research showed that low-cost applications with low maintenance required are best accepted [Tretiakov and Kinshuk, 2008].

An often-neglected issue is that the material offered is not attuned to learners' experience, expertise, and most of all their previous knowledge. It is important to acknowledge that distracting information and elements, which are not necessary to comprehend a concept, must be avoided as far as possible. The information provided to the learners must support the generation of appropriate mental models of the end-users. Moreover, the more complex and difficult the learning content is, the more important it is to direct cognitive and perceptual resources to intrinsic and germane processing [Holzinger et al., 2008], [Koper and Olivier, 2004], [Carroll and Mack, 1999], [Kinshuk and Sampson, 2004]. All these factors are important in contributing to learners' satisfaction, which is a critical success factor in mobile device development [Chen et al., 2008]. During development, it can be considered to include student modeling which can be seen as important process for the design of learning environments. Such learner models include for example information about the end-users such as domain competence, learning style or cognitive traits [Graf et al., 2008].

8.2.1 Related Work

At the Institute of Building Informatics of Graz University of Technology a wiki was used for lecturing and learning purposes for the first time in the beginning of 2005 [Ebner and Walder, 2008]. The aim was to support lectures like Computer Science I, Computer Science II and Structural Concrete by creating a knowledgebase for searching and retrieving information. Several studies were carried out to show how wiki-systems could be used for different learning processes [Ebner et al., 2006b], [Ebner et al., 2008], [Ebner and Walder, 2007]. Amongst others, students wrote an encyclopedia on civil engineering and there the problem of missing coordinates has been pointed out for the first time.

One example of the use of mobile technologies for teaching purposes is the EU project RAFT (Remote Accessible Field Trips), which was conducted from 2002 to 2005. The target of the project was the support of school classes with virtual excursions using portable Internet-conferencing tools [Kravcik et al., 2003]. In later stages the technology was incorporated in learning content management systems [Specht et al., 2005].

8.3 Requirements for TUGeoWiki

In order to cope with the previously defined requirements, a geowiki application was developed. The term *geowiki* is an already well established term which applies to geographically contextualized wikis [Priedhorsky et al., 2007]. While other geowiki implementations are usually focused on the geographical aspect and are implemented as editable maps[50], TUGeoWiki focuses on the description of the individual locations and the connections between them. The design of the TUGeoWiki server-side and client-side application was based on four central requirements, aiming to design a lightweight, geotagged and mobile application.

8.3.1 Why Lightweight, Geotagged and Mobile?

In order to combine the two aforementioned technological aspects, we designed and developed a solution approach for a *lightweight, geotagging-based* and *mobile* learning environment applying a geospatial wiki.

The term *lightweight* expresses our efforts to implement only the basic features of a geographical information system (GIS) for learning, namely (a) collecting, and (b) displaying geotagged data (also as map overlays). We consider further features of GIS, such as data analysis and modeling, to be out-of-scope, as they are only necessary for geosciences professionals. Moreover, our notion of *lightweight* embraces also our intent towards unobtrusive user interaction features based on well-known software practices. Especially as far as the technology acceptance of mobile applications is concerned, *lightweight* also refers to the overall costs, as low-cost applications with low maintenance efforts have turned out to be best accepted [Tretiakov and Kinshuk, 2008].

Further, our solution proposal concentrates on location-related information, and thus on learning scenarios where such information is an essential part of the curriculum. In those cases, students can benefit from a clearly defined relation of learning material to a geographic location (*geotagging-based*).

Finally, the term *mobile* describes our intention to offer access to information and learning material "in-the-field" in order to enhance "on-site learning" whenever applicable. It is worth stating at this point that within the context of our solution approach, we focus on mobile phones and PDAs[51] instead of other mobile technologies in order to stick with the primary goal of a lightweight system, as such devices are widespread and handy to carry in the field. Moreover, the user of mobile technology should enable us to foster collaborative activities of learners wherever possible, whenever possible.

8.3.2 Geotagging Interface

The first requirement was to provide a system which is based solely on geotagged information. Several available geotagging applications allow subsequent geotagging of existing images, which often leads to inaccurate or wrong coordinates. Such misplacements can usually be corrected, but require that the user realizes the mistake, performs an additional action, and is knowledgeable about the correct position.

In order to avoid such misplacements from the outset, the information added to TUGeoWiki must be properly geotagged. The two accepted alternatives to achieve this are the inclusion of the current location of the user (in a mobile setting) or the inclusion of the location stored within existing images (in a desktop setting). Both scenarios rely on a GPS receiver for providing information either about the current position or the position that should be included into the image files.

---

[51] PDA - Personal Digital Assistant

8.3.3 Mobile and Desktop Interface

The second requirement on the system is that it should be useful both while in the field and equally useful when post processing in a desktop environment. The first scenario makes it possible to retrieve information at the current location, upload images, and to create and edit location articles in the geowiki. Although information retrieval is a fundamental feature while the user is in the field, image upload and article editing are intended for limited use only, due to possible bandwidth restrictions, and due to the general usability restrictions of mobile phones as input devices.

The second scenario is focuses on discussion input, the batch uploading of images, report writing, adding location information articles, and information retrieval.

8.3.4 Collaborative Environment

In order to improve the impact on learning (in the desktop scenarios) a collaborative environment was identified as the third core requirement. Due to the positive results from its application to education (cf. i.e. [Fucks-Kittowski et al., 2004]), a wiki was chosen for this task. Although there are several other wiki systems available, we decided to use a Mediawiki[52]. Mediawiki is a software package, which was originally developed for Wikipedia. Mediawiki was chosen for two reasons.

First, it provides two well-defined mechanisms for extension of functionality: *special pages* and *templates*. *Special pages* are pages without Wiki content, which are generated on demand and are used to provide additional tools for users, e.g., file upload [Mediawiki, 2008b]. *Templates* are pages created for transclusion purposes, and usually contain repetitive materials or blocks of information (e.g., infoboxes) [Mediawiki, 2008a].

---

[52] http://www.mediawiki.org/wiki/MediaWiki/de, accessed 2009-04-22

Secondly, the user interface of MediaWiki is probably the best-known Wiki user interface, among others, due to the immensely broad use and high popularity of Wikipedia [Voelkel and Oren, 2006]. Moreover, this decision was supported by the fact that Mediawiki is free software and therefore can be modified to fit the requirements for TUGeoWiki.

8.3.5 Map Mashup

The final requirement was to provide the integration of external location-based material based on the coordinates available for location articles in the TUGeoWiki. This enables the integration of highly detailed material from external sources without the need to provide such material within the TUGeoWiki itself, a concept known as a mashup. The term was coined by the music community and was used to describe when vocals and music from different songs were mixed to produce a new sound. In technology, the term refers to applications that combine contents from different sources and present them to the users seamlessly. The most obvious use for a mashup in TUGeoWiki's case would be to integrate mapping material using an API such as the Google Maps API[53]. Numerous other map APIs are available and the integration of further material, such as geological data, could be considered.

8.4 Development of the TUGeoWiki Application

Our solution approach, the TUGeoWiki system, is a geospatial Web-based mobile application that aims at supporting the learning scenarios given so far. The final TUGeoWiki application consists of two independent systems that fulfill the requirements detailed above. Most of the interaction is performed using a Web application (a Mediawiki, with specially developed extensions) within a mobile and/or desktop browser. In order to make this extended functionality available on a mobile

---

[53] http://maps.google.com, accessed 2009-04-22

device in the field, an additional mobile client was implemented. Furthermore, as detailed above, several external applications were included in the final mashup.

TUGeoWiki modifies the MediaWiki paradigm of *pages* for the individual entries in order to define *places,* which are associated with geographical coordinates, and thus represent real-world *locations.* In our terminology the term *place* thus defines the entity in the system, while the term *location* denotes the actual geographical entity.

This modification is achieved by using MediaWiki's *special pages* to create location-based entries as well as templates to display them. Figure 3 depicts the concept of creating a *place.* These templates are designed as mashups, thus extending the Wiki entries with mapping material from Google Maps or Microsoft Live Search Maps. Additionally, a hyperlink to the MediaWiki extension *Geohack* provides access to numerous other map sources [Wikipedia, 2008].

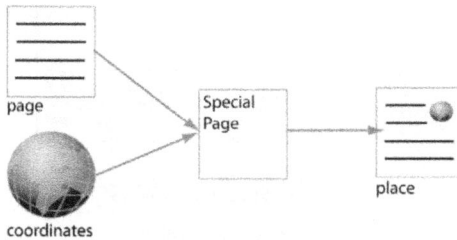

Figure 3: General notion for creating places in TUGeoWiki

Figure 8-4 depicts the components of the desktop application scenario and the interaction flow within them. On the client side, all of the interaction is done with a browser, which connects to a Mediawiki on the TUGeoWiki server. The original Mediawiki has been extended with two special pages. The first offers a list of all geotagged articles in the wiki. More specifically, this page implements the functionality for the creation of new locations based on geographical coordinates. The second special page supports the image inclusion coordinates.

Within JPEG images, additional information can be stored in a so-called EXIF header [Japan Electronics an Information Technology Industries Association, 2002]. Besides metadata regarding a broad range of standard information such as date, time, or camera model, the EXIF header may also contain the geographical coordinates of the image. This information can either be added with a camera, when a photo is taken, or added later. In order for the camera to be able to do this, it must have access to a (built-in) GPS receiver, such as the Ricoh 500SE camera or the Nokia N-95 mobile phone. To add this information to the JPEG later, the user's coordinates must be recorded using a separate GPS tracker such as the Holux M-241 Datalogger while the photo was taken. The coordinate information can be later merged with the images based on the image's and GPS coordinate's timestamps.

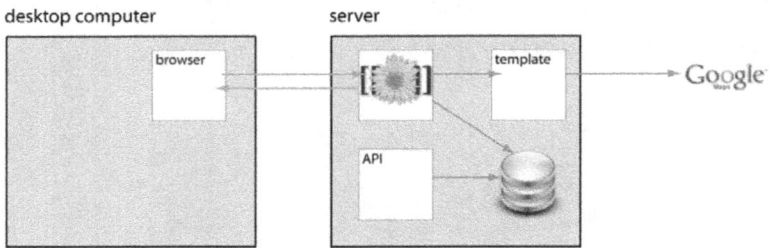

Figure 8-4: Desktop scenario

The mobile scenario extends the desktop scenario by integrating an additional application which is on the mobile device, as depicted in Figure 8-5. This application is responsible for accessing an internal or external GPS receiver and for relaying these coordinates to the TUGeoWiki application opened in the mobile phone's browser. For compatibility reasons the *Java Platform, Micro Edition*[54] (J2ME) was chosen for the initial development of this application. The application itself was designed using a model-view-controller pattern. It provides features to access the current location, take an image and integrate this location, search for location articles in a radius of 10-100 meters around the current position, and to upload images on the TUGeoWiki server.

---

[54] http://java.sun.com/javame/index.jsp, accessed 2008-08-04

Upon uploading an image, the user may then search for existing locations within a 10 to 100-metre radius of the coordinates embedded in the image. The image can subsequently be added to an existing location article, or a new article stub can be created containing just this image and a *template* (previously described). This article stub can later be expanded, either in the mobile or desktop scenario. As mentioned above, the uploading of images, which are not geotagged is not permitted by the system in order to restrict the information contained in location articles to properly geotagged information.

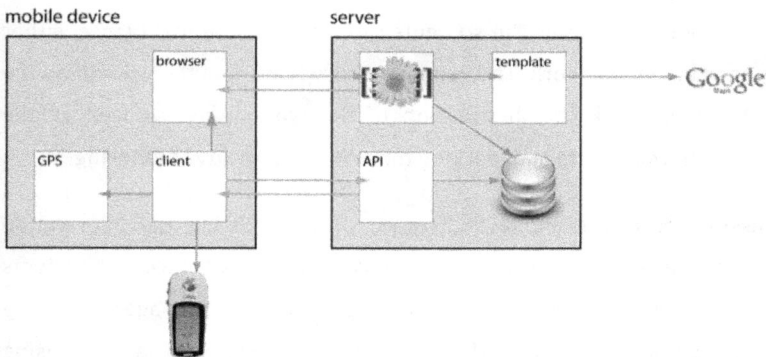

Figure 8-5: Mobile scenario

The same restriction also affects the search for existing location articles. If no article within the chosen radius can be found, the user is presented with the option to create a new article stub containing only a location name and a *template* for further expansion.

8.5 Learning Scenarios

The first successful evaluations in the course of civil engineering excursions revealed, beside potential improvements, the need for a closer inspection of possible learning scenarios with a geospatial wiki in higher education. These scenarios are used to describe possible applications of the geowiki and their impact on the learning process.

8.5.1 Generic e-learning Scenarios

TUGeoWiki is designed to be used in e-learning scenarios without a mobile learning component. In this case, the Web application is used *per se*, abandoning the mobile application. The two main scenarios for this application are yet again focused on the support of field trips.

The first possible example is the preparation of students for such a field trip. In various situations, it is preferable that students have already prepared information concerning the locations they are going to visit. Teachers may create *place stubs* in the wiki; short articles already geotagged for a certain location, but containing little of no further information but the location's title. The students can extend these in advance, either collaboratively or in individual work. The version history feature of the wiki offers the teacher possibilities to check the distribution of the work done, as well as the individual participants work parts and working times in collaborative authoring.

The second possible generic example focuses on post-processing the information gained on a field trip. Again, teachers may prepare *place stubs* in advance and students may compile information about the individual locations. Moreover, images can easily be added to the final *places* in the wiki, if they are geotagged. An alternative to using the mobile TUGeoWiki application *in the field* is the application of a geo tracker. This external device logs geographical coordinates to timestamps. Later on, these tracks can be used to post-process images taken by synchronizing the coordinates of the track with the image creation times. Available software can be used to add the coordinates into the images' EXIF header information. These geotagged images can be uploaded to TUGeoWiki and used to find fitting *places* in the wiki.

8.5.2 Generic m-Learning Scenarios

As previously mentioned, one of the core concepts of TUGeoWiki is to be used *in the field*. The principal learning scenario in this context is the use of mobile devices like mobile phones to access the TUGeoWiki application. These mobile devices are used to retrieve the coordinates of the current location and access existing *places* in TUGeoWiki in arbitrary vicinity. As such, the application is used to retrieve background information about the current location (i.e. compiled by a teacher beforehand) and made accessible to provide spatially contextual information. The students can use this information during the process of learning in order to better understand relations of a location to theoretical concepts or other locations [Lonsdale et al., 2004].

The second learning scenario in the mobile context is the application of TUGeoWiki for the compilation of information about real-world locations by the students. On the one hand, textual information can be added to existing or newly created *places*. On the other hand, the device can be used to create geotagged images of a location and add them to a *place* in TUGeoWiki. In this scenario, the creation of *place-stubs* in TUGeoWiki by the teacher beforehand is advisable to provide a core skeleton of the intended structure. The impact on the learning process in this scenario lies in the compilation of the information itself, the digestion of the direct experience gained during the field trip and the informal learning during this task [Specht et al., 2005].

This second scenario can be extended by a collaborative component. The features of the wiki allow several students to work on the same *places* and collaborate in the compilation of information. The learning process is enhanced by discussions and the need to create a unified perspective on the location. The change history of the wiki provides means for personal accountability of the students for their part in the final work, a central prerequisite for effective cooperative learning [Johnson and Johnson, 1994]. The advantage of this scenario is that the students can do their work on the actual locations concerned. Alternative scenarios, with one part of the collaborating students *in situ* and another part working remotely, as proposed by [Kravcik et al., 2003], can also be implemented with TUGeoWiki.

8.5.3 Limitations

While the first evaluations carried out by lecturers on excursions have shown a positive perception of the e-learning scenarios, especially the m-learning scenarios face several limitations. One of the main limitations is the need for mobile devices providing GPS service and Internet access for all students. Although some of the students already have access to suiting equipment, this can still pose a problem for the majority.

Figure 8-6: Example *place* from the first field study

8.6 Experimental Setting and Methods: Field Studies

8.6.1 Initial Evaluation of Field Trip Post-Processing

In the course of the evaluation of TUGeoWiki three concrete scenarios were successively developed. After the initial development of the geowiki approach was evaluated in a field trip of civil engineers, applying a variant of the second e-learning scenario (field trip post-processing). In this scenario, the lecturer was equipped with a

Nokia N95[55] mobile phone, supplying an internal GPS receiver, and the TUGeoWiki mobile application. The lecturer was asked to use the phone to create geotagged images of the field trip, which were subsequently uploaded to TUGeoWiki and assigned to *places*. In this scenario, TUGeoWiki was solely used as an application to create and provide geotagged learning material. Figure 8-6 depicts the *place* created for a sample location in this scenario.

8.6.1.1 Evaluation results

Due to the fact that in the first step geotagged pictures were only taken by the lecturer, a short interview took place to gain his first impressions. Furthermore, also the limits and potentials of the software were carried out.

Following crucial factors can be pointed out:

- Geotagging by mobile phone: From a technical point of view the lecturer reported that using the mobile phone for taking geotagged pictures was easy. Only waiting for the GPS-signal for the first time seemed to be cumbersomely in the same way as losing the signal indoors. In such cases, manual geotagging or using the last coordinates may overcome this situation.

- Easy upload: The user also mentioned that the upload to the TUGeoWiki was easy and encouraged using the system. Due to the fact that each file must be uploaded one by one, a bulk upload of high number of files should be realized.

- Number of mobile phones with built-in GPS: One problem in the future will be that of course not each student will own a mobile phone with built-in GPS and to wait that it becomes standardized will take some time. Especially for collaboration, all pictures of the lecturers and learners should be gathered to present many different details seen on-site. With

[55] http://www.nokiausa.com/link?cid=PLAIN_TEXT_430087, accessed 2009-04-22

the help of a GPS tracker this situation should improve. The lecturer would record the location automatically in predefined time steps. Afterwards using valid time stamps all collected pictures would be synchronized with global coordinates.

⊕ Radius-depended upload: The lecturer pointed out that the radius-depended upload was extremely useful. By defining a radius (currently between 10-100 meters), all pictures within this distance were placed within one wiki page. Especially in the case when pictures of an object from different views and places were taken, TUGeoWiki allowed to put it one instead of several pages. Concerning the dimension of building sites this was a necessary feature to avoid a huge amount of pictures anywhere in the system that belong to one place. Otherwise, it will be possible to show different construction stages as well as different contract sections. In case of road works or hydraulic building sites this will be of high importance

⊕ Geological information: Another advantage of providing global coordinates for an object is that also geological information is available as well as hydraulic data. From a didactical point of view, the lecturer can visualize the complex coherences between an object and its surrounding environment.

⊕ Collaboration: using the TUGeoWiki for writing, the students' reports should enhance collaboration in thefuture. Furthermore, by collecting a high number of pictures of different building sites a database for teaching can be established.

In the end, it should be pointed out that though several images could not be extended with geographical coordinates (because they were indoor scenarios) and the study was restricted to a non-collaborative scenario, the feedback from the instructor confirmed the usefulness of TUGeoWiki approach for the intended application.

8.6.2 Evaluation in a Collaborative Scenario

As a second concrete experiment, the second e-learning scenario (collaborative post-processing of field trips) was implemented for another civil engineering field trip in a follow-up study. The students were equipped with a mixed technological equipment of digital cameras and one Nokia N95. The teacher was furthermore equipped with a Holux M-241[56] external GPS tracker and the students asked to synchronize the time settings of the cameras with the data tracker. Images for the creation of the field trip report were taken collaboratively throughout the trip and subsequently geotagged using the GPS track. The resulting image set was uploaded on TUGeoWiki and relayed to the *places* created for the field trip. One-on-one interviews were conducted with the participants of the field trip to investigate the user experience with this scenario.

8.6.3 Evaluation of Collaborative Field Trip Preparation

The third concrete scenario implemented for the evaluation of TUGeoWiki focused on a geology field trip. TUGeoWiki was used by the students in the preparation of the trip. The scenario combines the first generic e-learning scenario (trip preparation) with the third generic m-learning scenario (collaborative work *in the field*). The preparation of this scenario revealed the need for an extension of TUGeoWiki's content paradigm. While the previous experiments had shown the basic usefulness of the *place* paradigm in a civil engineering scenario, which is focused on building sites, geologists have extended the requirements, as information can rarely be mapped to individual locations. The two additional paradigms of *areas* and *tracks* need to be supported. An *area* is represented by a polygon on a map and is useful for the description of larger-scale geological conditions. A *track* is represented by a line connecting a number of locations and describes an actual sequence of locations visited in the course of the trip. These additional paradigms are currently in the course of being implemented for evaluation.

---

[56] http://www.holux.com/JCore/en/products/products_content.jsp?pno=341, accessed 2009-04-22

As far as the concrete scenario is concerned, a set of *place stubs* was created and prepared for the field trip. The *places* have been summarized into a wiki category, and are collaboratively expanded by groups of students. During the field trip, the group would be equipped with digital cameras, a mobile device and the GPS tracker. On the one hand, the mobile device will be used to add information *in the field* and thus extend the previously prepared articles. On the other hand, the images will subsequently be geotagged, uploaded and added to the existing *places* in order to enrich them with visual information from the actual trip. Figure 8-7 depicts the collection of the prepared *place stubs*.

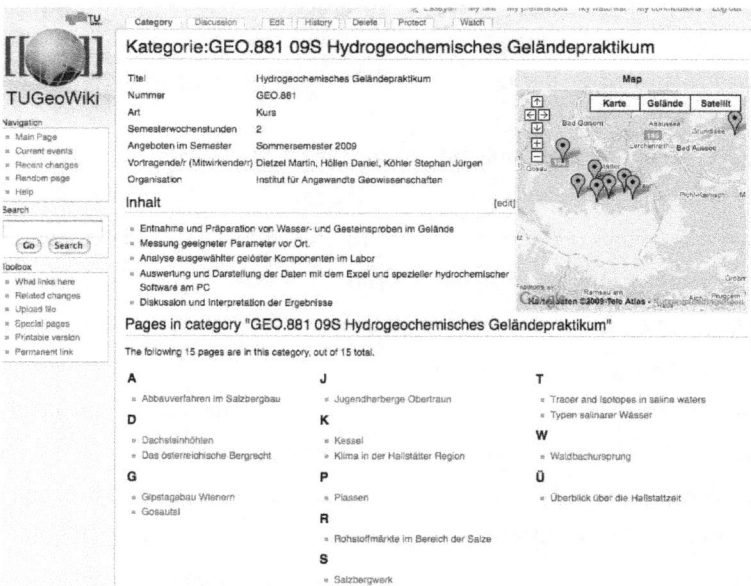

Figure 8-7: Preparation material for a geological field trip prepared with TUGeoWiki

8.7 Microblog Integration

In the previous chapter, the two possible application scenarios for TUGeowiki, mobile and desktop, have been described. It has been shown that the mobile scenario is mainly focused on the satisfaction of ad-hoc learning needs as well as on a proactive information push to the wiki, rather than on collaborative editing of contents. So far, the examples given for such an information push were the creation of *place stubs* and the extension of *places* with geotagged images.

However, this approach lacks a possibility to easily share information about/across images via the mobile application. For any textual information added to individual locations, the standard Mediawiki edit functionality must be accessed with the mobile browser.

First evaluations with a small group of users showed that this functionality was perceived as cumbersome and avoided as far as possible. These reactions of the evaluation subjects are assumed to be a result of the typical mobile phones limitations regarding their small screen sizes and the complexity of writing with mobile or virtual keyboards. In order to solve this problem and to simplify the interactions with the wiki, we propose the usage of an alternative technique, which is based on the principle of adding (small) notes to existing articles as a foundation for collaborative activities within our desktop application scenario. In analogy to the *Microblog* paradigm [Templeton, 2008], short messages are sent by the users and integrated into the wiki, creating *Micropages*.

8.7.1 The Notion of Micropages

Due to the fact that the number of mobile devices connected to the World Wide Web is growing incredibly fast, microblogging has become one of the most interesting innovative applications nowadays. Microblogging can be seen as a variant of blogging, where small messages, usually not longer than 140 characters, are posted instantly and on-demand to microblogging service. Microblogging can be defined as *"a small-*

scale form of blogging, generally made up of short, succinct messages, used by both consumers and businesses to share news, post status updates, and carry on conversation" [Templeton, 2008]. As far as the user intentions are concerned, these intentions can be categorized in the following four types: daily chatter, conversations, sharing information, and reporting news [Java et al., 2007]. Further, research work has pointed out that microblogging is extremely useful for the fast exchange of thoughts, ideas and information sharing [Ebner and Schiefner, 2008]. Considering the growing importance of mobility and mobile applications, Twitter (the largest microblogging platform worldwide) became one of the prime examples for Mobile 2.0 [Griswold, 2007].

To characterize the notion of wiki pages that are based on small individual information pushes, we apply the term *micropages*. Thus, micropages are the wiki analogy of microblogs. This fact describes that our approach focuses on smaller parts of information.

In a microblog, brief text updates are used as status messages to publish information for friends and other "followers". By encouraging shorter posts, microblogging can fulfil a need for a faster form of communication [Java et al., 2007]. Within the scope of this chapter, we propose to use micropages as wiki pages that are built out of short individual annotations on the topic of the *page*. In TUGeowiki, each of these topics is a location, and each page is a *place*. Figure 8-8 depicts one example of a micropage in TUGeowiki containing one annotation.

The creation process of such a micropage by means of the wiki's special pages is depicted in Figure 8-9. A short message is created (usually on a mobile device) and geotagged with the user's current location. A special page is used to find an appropriate *place* or create a new one, and to append the message at the end of the micropage.

Figure 8-8: Example of a TUGeowiki *micropage* with one annotation

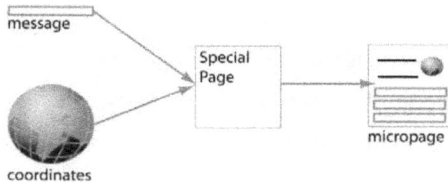

Figure 8-9: General notion for creating micropages

The building parts of a TUGeowiki micropage are derived from the received messages and always appended in chronological order (earliest on top) instead of in reverse chronological order (as in weblogs) to better address the wiki page paradigm. These parts are furthermore tagged with some metadata, such as the author's username, the date and time of the post.

Unlike microblogs, micropages are not intended to serve as means of synchronous communication, but to share only the concept of information push of short messages. Further, a new micropage is not intended to represent a final content in the wiki; rather (as for wiki contents in general) it should be iteratively revised and improved to a final form via collaborative authoring. In concrete, micropages represent stubs for content in a wiki, i.e., short annotations added to "sketch" the final page anytime, anywhere, and in the case of TUGeowiki *in-the-field* and *just-in-time*.

8.7.2 Using Micropages with the Mobile Client

Micropages are currently supported by TUGeoWiki's Android and Symbian clients. In both versions, the annotation attached to a micropage has been implemented for the upload of pictures. This process is described in the following.

In a first step, the user writes a message of 140 characters at most, annotating her current location and chooses a distance from the current location for the search of suitable existing *places*. The client subsequently retrieves the current position from the built-in GPS sensor and relays it to the server, which returns the list of existing places within the chosen distance. On the client-side, the user chooses either one of the existing *places* to annotate or creates a new *place* by entering a title. As previously mentioned, the message is then attached at the end of the *place*, accompanied by the user's username as well as the date and time of the post.

Some sample screenshots of the TUGeowiki Android client during the annotation workflow are shown in Figure 8-10. The second screenshot shows the selection of the distance for searching existing *places*. The third screenshot displays the list of existing *places* retrieved. Finally, the fourth screenshot displays the message included in one of these *places*, in the wiki at server side.

Figure 8-11 displays the corresponding workflow on the iPhone application. In the first screenshot, on the left side of the figure, a message is composed. The second screenshot displays the selection of the appropriate radius, while the third screenshots depicts the corresponding list of *places* in the wiki. Finally, the last screenshot depicts the map of places in the vicinity of the user's current location.

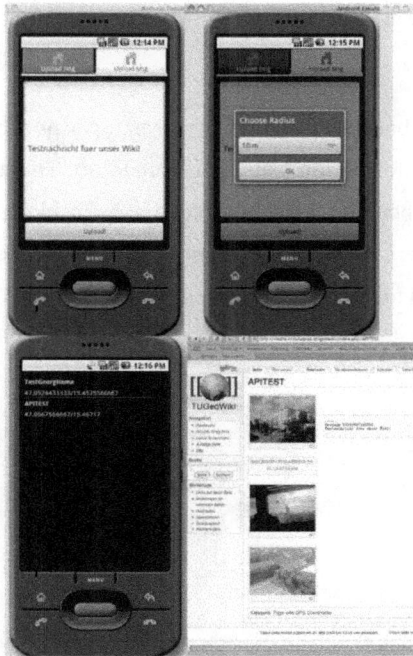

Figure 8-10: Screenshots of the annotation feature in the mobile client

8.7.3 Integrating Microblogging Services

Another possible source for the creation of micropages is the integration of a so-called *microblogging service*. The analogy of micropages and microblogs inspired us to define an additional user interface. As stated earlier in this chapter, the *annotation* feature of the mobile client is merely intended for in-the-field and just-in-time annotations of geospatial information by sending short messages that describe the current location.

Due to the fact that the location is determined via GPS coordinates, a later annotation of resources is not feasible. The problem in this context arises when short annotations to already existing wiki places are interesting for users *after* visiting the location, thus the following alternative user interaction might be of interest. In TUGeowiki we integrated microblogging services that support Twitter posts. We have chosen the

Twitter service because it is a well-known microblogging application with a well-defined API.

Taking into account this background, a very interesting aspect of microblogging gained our attention: filtering information using a unique letter. This technique is referred to as *hash tagging* and has been introduced on several microblogging platforms. It is used for search queries or marking special content. *Hashtags* are a simple way of grouping messages with a "#" sign followed by a name or special code. [23]

Figure 8-11: Screenshot of annotation feature of the mobile iPhone client

Hashtags in microblogs are especially meaningful when used during a particular period of time, as *"it not only allows individuals to generate a resource based on that specific thematic, while using the hashtag, but also bridges knowledge, and knowing, across networks of interest"*. [Reinhardt et al., 2009]

On the server side of the TUGeowiki system, users may use a special page to mark a *place* as "microbloggable". Moreover, individual users are provided a feature to append their Twitter user names to their user profiles. This information is relayed to a Web service, which periodically scans the registered users' microblogs for tweets containing the hashtag "#tgw", indicating a TUGeowiki annotation message. This tweet must contain a second hashtag identifying the place via an URL. This hashtag is created using the URL shortening service bit.ly, which creates a 5-letter hash of an URL.

The URL http://media.iicm.tugraz.at/geowiki/index.php/LKH_Klagenfurt_Neu, for example, results in the URL http://bit.ly/jBVbX. The corresponding hashtag, #jBVbX, is created for a place when marking it "microbloggable" and added to the TUGeowiki template.

After identifying the TUGeowiki-specific hashtags, the remainder of the Twitter post is added to the corresponding TUGeowiki place as a new annotation signed with the corresponding user name, date and time.

8.8 Conclusion

Mobile phones with built-in electronic magnetic compasses have been available for some time (e.g. the Nokia 5140), but not in combination with a GPS sensor. Together, these two sensors would allow us to determine not only where a picture was taken, but also the direction in which the device or person was pointing, i.e., which building was actually being photographed. This of course, would significantly enhance the usefulness and quality of the tags attached to a given picture.

From a didactical point of view, the use of the TUGeoWiki in learning and teaching scenarios must be researched to discover further potentials. Main buildings as well as famous ones can be described, located and discussed in a more collaborative way. Lecturers have to change their role towards a more steering and leading one.

However, subsequently the impact of this additional data has to be tested by using it in real-life scenarios. Other departments like architecture or medicine are currently getting involved in the project. First experiments showed the potential use of TUGeoWiki for archeological surveys, and in the context of medicine, TUGeoWiki can act as a geospatially enhanced medical wiki.

Chapter 9 Outlook

On the next pages of this book, an approach to outline future development in the context of social media, technology-enhanced learning, and the intersection of both will be given. Several issues currently gaining importance in this field will be discussed, and a future development, as seen from a current point of view, will be sketched.

9.1 Status quo - Social Media, Web 2.0, and E-Learning 2.0 at Universities in 2009

Based on the initial survey on the use of Social Web technologies in Education presented in Chapter 4, a follow-up study has been conducted in June 2009 to validate the changes in these three years. The participants of this study were 47 students of various computer science curricula at Graz University of Technology. Eight of the participants were female. The questions were based on the initial survey, though slightly modified to cope with unclear answers. Moreover, Microblogging was included as an application.

9.1.1 Results

In order to match the questions of the first survey in 2006, the knowledge about the set of Social Web applications of interest was investigated in a preliminary step. As the vast majority of the participants of the first survey had indicated that they knew the applications in question, this possible answer has been refined to the two levels "known" and "well known". Table 9-1 displays the results of this question

Table 9-1: Knowledge about Applications

	Weblogs	Wikis	Micro-blogging	Audio Podcasts	Video Podcasts	Virtual Worlds	Media Sharing
Well known	42,6%	59,6%	10,6%	34,0%	40,4%	17,0%	44,7%
Known	44,7%	29,8%	25,5%	38,3%	36,2%	23,4%	25,5%
Not Sure	10,6%	8,5%	42,6%	23,4%	21,3%	51,1%	23,4%
Unknown	0,0%	0,0%	19,1%	0,0%	0,0%	6,4%	4,3%
No Answer	2,1%	2,1%	2,1%	4,3%	2,1%	2,1%	2,1%

Still weblogs and wikis turned out to be the best-known applications in the survey. In contrast to the first survey, none of the participants stated that weblogs, wikis, and podcasts were totally unknown to them. Microblogging, as a relatively new Social Medium, was the least known application in the field.

Subsequently the applications were analyzed for their use frequencies in passive use, authoring, learning, and guided educational settings. Figure 9-1 displays the passive use frequencies, indicating reading or consuming use of the applications. Figure 9-2 displays the frequencies for authoring, providing and publishing content. Figure 9-3 indicates the frequencies for self-paced learning scenarios including these social media applications. Figure 9-4, finally, indicates the frequency of use in lectures and other educational settings guided by a teacher or educator.

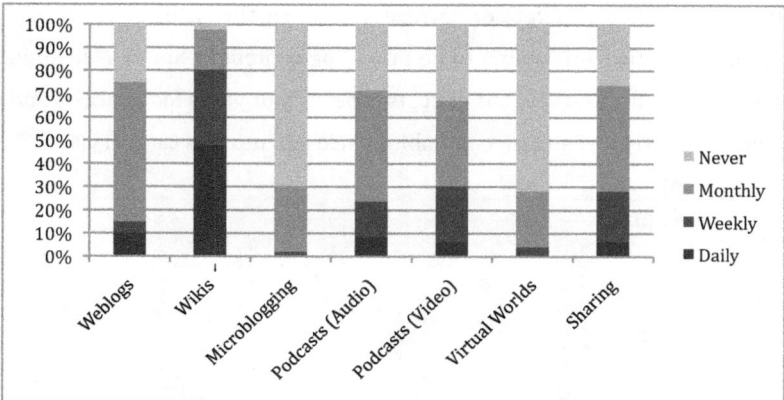

Figure 9-1: Use Frequency of Applications

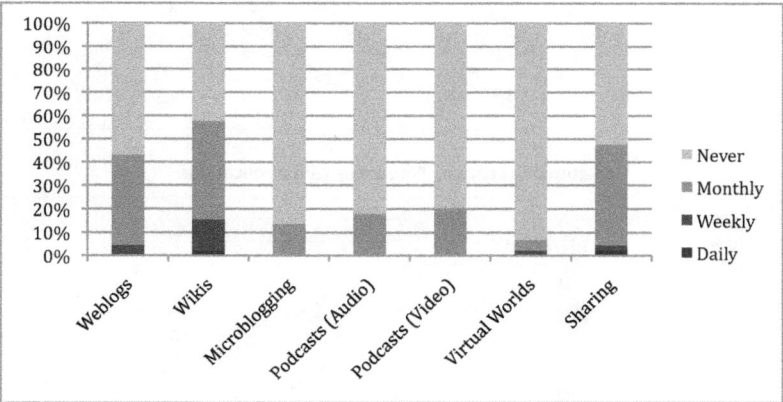

Figure 9-2: Authoring Frequency with Applications

Interestingly, the use frequencies differ from those found in the first survey. Though, as could be predicted due to the increased familiarity with the applications, the rate of students who *never* use certain applications decreased for all social media in the set, the rates for frequent use, defined as weekly or daily use, also decreased.

This decrease is especially striking in the context of weblogs. Still 75% of the participants read weblogs at least monthly. Yet, only 14%, as opposed to 51% in 2006, read weblogs at least weekly. Investigation of the reasons for this development should be the focus of subsequent surveys.

Matching the well-known effect of participation inequality [Hill et al., 1992], only a minority of the participants stated to be providing content in Social Web applications regularly. As in the first survey, this effect is especially obvious for podcasts and virtual worlds, yet the newly investigated microblogs also fall into this category.

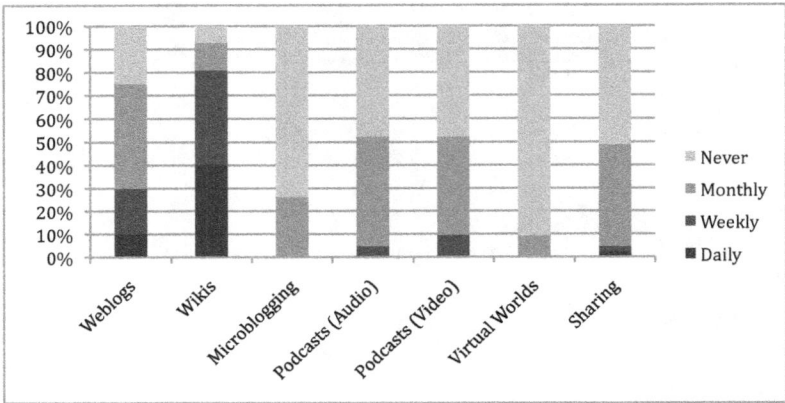

Figure 9-3: Learning Frequency with Applications

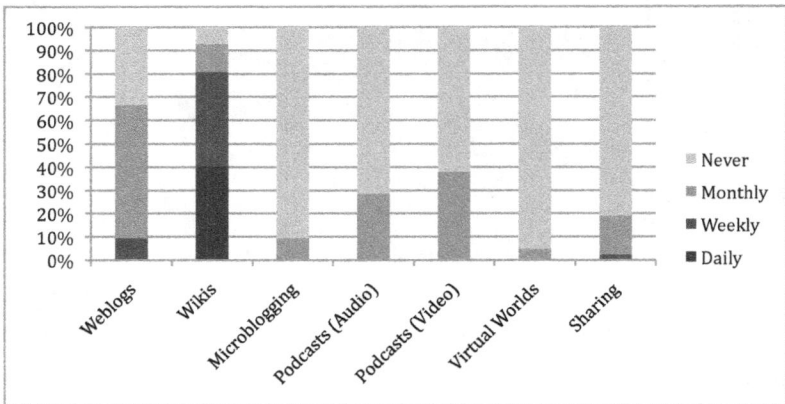

Figure 9-4: Teaching Frequency with Applications

As far as the application to self-paced learning activities is concerned, wikis still are the most frequently used social media. Many of the participants use weblogs at least monthly, but the part of the participants using them more frequently decreased in comparison to 2006. The same effect is obvious for podcasts.

Lecturers still apply wikis in the context of lectures most frequently. Weblogs are used regularly, but not as frequently as in 2006. The other social media applications in the survey set were also used regularly by a small group of the participants, yet none of them on a weekly or more frequent basis.

Summarizing the status quo, social media have become a part of the lives of students during the last years. They are used on a regular basis, although not as frequently as at the beginning of the hype cycle in the middle of the decade. Still there are manifold possibilities to apply social media to enhance informal learning in technology-enhanced learning and teaching.

9.2 Web-Based Systems and Scalability Issues

Forthcoming learning systems based on Web technology will also require change in their architectural design to cope with growing numbers of users and alternative usage scenarios. Service oriented Architecture (SoC) has been credited to be one possible solution in this context.

9.2.1 Factors Effecting Scalability

Scalability defines the behaviors in growing or more demanding environments. For Web applications, scalability specifies the response or ability to perform expected operations on larger scale. Larger scale may refer to expansion in terms of users, data, services, operation domain, and hardware.

One possible approach to make technology-enhanced learning systems scalable is the support of vertical scalability where response is controlled with the expansion of system within a single logical unit. The second possible approach is the support of horizontal scalability, which refers to expansion as multiple logical units working as a single entity.

Because of the current nature of Web based learning environments, horizontal scalability is the prime concern. The factors effecting horizontal scalability include the ability to leverage open industry standards, as well as the use of flexible technology to include different systems and data structures. It also requires a generic interface for clients to provide broader coverage. However, most importantly it needs a good controlling mechanism for the integration of resources.

Although addition of horizontal scalability to a system does not require addition of expensive hardware for larger operations, it also saves the effort for building a structure and storage of a combined knowledge space. However in order to achieve successful horizontal scaling, applications must be built using a specific architecture. This architecture must support a network files system (for scalability of he data layer), distributed computing and load balancing at the application layer.

9.2.2 Web Scale Virtual Computing Environments

During the last few years, the Web has been transformed into a distributed and global application platform. Web sites and applications are turning increasingly into Web services that allow information exchange with other systems in addition to information provision to user. A major factor that transformed web into a platform for distributed computing is the use of XML. XML describes structured data in standard plain text rather than any application specific representations. This enabled Web applications to share and store data globally, providing the foundation for developing loosely coupled applications. The first generation of these distributed Web applications was based on a number of data transport and integration mechanisms like Distributed Component Object Model (DCOM), Enterprise JavaBeans (EJB) and Common Object Request Broker Architecture (CORBA). What really boosted these Web based computing environments is the use of universal connectivity in form of web services [Coyle, 2002]. Web services provide interoperable machine-to-machine interaction over WWW. Based on standardized and platform independent protocols, they help in building distributed and collaborative Web applications.

Emerging learning applications are starting to empower themselves by adding facilities of inter-application communication over the Web. This comes in form of dissemination and consumption of syndicated contents, use of unified user authentication, search and retrieval facilities across distributed databases. The application of a scalable service based approach can be seen as the last component of an idea for technology-enhanced learning in a *learning web* perceived by Illich as early as the 70s [Illich, 1971].

9.3 Privacy Issues

Another upcoming issue concerning social media, and especially social network sites, that will affect the future development in this area, is the question of privacy. Phishing and identity theft have become grave concern of users [Staddon, 2009]. As in the case of all highly personalized systems, the question which users have access to the individual parts of the information available is the key concern. This multifaceted problem gains increased complexity due to the fact that users may want to share certain information with a distinct part of the community (i.e. family and close friends), but not with the community as a whole [Gross et al., 2005].

Another frequent privacy breach concerns the community building features of social media sites. Features, which should facilitate the formation of a community by suggesting new contacts for the users can easily turn into privacy traps. Such suggestions can be based on profile attributes (i.e. not publically available attributes), or be mined from email, address book, or text messaging histories [Staddon, 2009].

Usually, social network sites provide possibilities to restrict the access to certain types of personal information for different groups of contacts. However, a remaining concern for the users is the fact of possible leaks of sensitive data, which is stored a social media sites. Such leaks may on the one hand arise from misuse based on privacy disclosure. On the other hand they may result from attacks, or cross-site data mining [Chen and Shi, 2009].

These concerns for privacy are even more prominent in the context of technology-enhanced learning, due to the sensitivity of information on learning performance and assessment. Privacy statements offer little help due to the lack of common language between lawyers and users. One possible solution is the application of a privacy framework as proposed by [Garcia-Barrios et al., 2009], in order to provide a methodical approach to give the user control over privacy settings.

Another possible approach, especially in the context of social media applications in education, is to refrain from using publically accessible social media applications. Instead, institutional setups of social media services could be used, which are not publically accessible, but are restricted to the communities of learners involved. These approaches could also be included in an institutional LMS [Notess, 2009].

9.4 Social Networks meet Collaborative Tools

One of the basic reasons for the success of social networks is the need to stay in touch and communicate. Social networks provide tools like messaging services or instant messaging for that end. On the other side, collaborative applications provide means of visualizing the users' own networks and contacts, and communicate with them.

In 2009, Google announced a tool to bridge the gap between social networks and collaborative tools. Google Wave[57] is described as "an online tool for real-time communication and collaboration". It is aimed to provide a unified solution to manage the own social networks, communicate with the own contacts and collaborate on documents.

The announcement of Google Wave created a buzz in the media and the blogosphere. First videos indicated interesting technology and new paradigms of communications. This hype was increased due to the fact of a closed beta, with only some 100.000 invitations available. In the meantime, though, a lot of the early participants stopped using the Google Wave beta [Douglis, 2010]. One of the problems in this context could

---

[57] https://wave.google.com/, accessed 2010-03-15

be the limited size of the community, which, according to Metcalfe's Law also limits the usefulness of the network [Shapiro and Varian, 1999]. Moreover, the beta still has some drawbacks, which limit the usefulness.

9.4.1 Current drawbacks of Google Wave

The communication in Google Wave is based on individual *waves*, which are the summary of all input of the participants. One of the major issues is based on the fact of modifiability of these waves. Any user may edit any part of a wave, even the input of another user. These changes are not obviously labeled. It is possible to retrace all modifications by a *replay* feature, which presents the history of all actions within a wave, but in long waves, finding the exact modification searched can be time consuming.

Another problem with the user interface is the fact that by default the other participants of a wave see user's input in real-time. This means that each letter typed is transmitted and displayed immediately, which can be quite distracting, or, in some situations, even embarrassing.

Another major issue is the fact, that a wave looks identical for all participants. This means i.e. that the automatic translation, which can be applied, translates the content for all participants, an approach with a doubtful usefulness in a multilingual environment.

9.4.2 Future Impact

Aside from all previously mentioned issues of the early versions, Google Wave still provides a novel approach to the communication with communities of interest or practice. One of the main reasons for its presumable success is the fact that the Wave server and Wave client are independent developments. Most of the drawbacks stated before only refer to the Wave client, which could always be replaced by alternative clients. The underlying server paradigm, in contrast, allows radically innovative classes of applications. The important factor for Google Wave in this context will be to keep hold of early adopters.

Chapter 10   Summary and Conclusions

Within the course of this book, the importance of social media concepts in the context of contemporary educational approaches has been explained. The subsequent chapter recapitulates the outcome of the research presented in this book. The individual scenarios for the application of social media in technology-enhanced learning are summarized.

10.1 Research Results

Based on a set of research questions proposed at the beginning of this book, a set of scenarios has been developed to provide answers for these questions. Moreover, exemplary applications have been implemented to suit these scenarios. The results of this research are summarized in the following pages.

10.1.1   Familiarity with Social Media Applications and Technologies

The two fundamental questions on social media and learning concern the familiarity of the students with these technologies and the dissemination of social media in learning and teaching. These very basic research questions was initially answered a survey conducted in 2006, identifying the status quo. Students had a high level of familiarity with the better-known applications of Web 2.0, like wikis and weblogs. Yet, they lacked knowledge about more recent trends. Moreover, only a minority of the students was actively publishing content in Web 2.0. Leaving aside wikis, the students had very limited contact with social media tools in the context of education.

10.1.2   The Correlation of Social Media Activity and Learning Performance

In the research for the two preliminary research questions, the fact that students up to now focus the application of social media primarily on wikis and weblogs has been affirmed. Due to this high popularity, weblogs were chosen as a social media tool for the evaluation of possible correlation of the activity within social media and the learning performance of the students.

Following the constructivist learning approach, weblogs can be applied as learning logs in educational settings to recapitulate learning progress and open questions. This setting was applied to the context of a software development lecture. As far as the education in programming languages is concerned, weblogs seem especially well suited due to the impact on reflection on the own work and thus continuous engagement with the learning content.

The students' activity in their weblogs has been shown to be a good overall predictor of the performance of the students in the example programming tasks in the investigated lecture. The students applied their weblogs to post a broad variety of lecture related content, but to a large part concentrated on the recapitulation of their own progress and performance in programming.

10.1.3   Social Media applied for the Externalization of Knowledge in a Community of Learners

A collaborative online mind-mapping tool has been developed to support brainstorming and visualization tasks in technology-enhanced learning. Key features to support educational scenarios are the traceability of the individual collaborative input by the users, as well as the possibility to support local and distant collaborative scenarios.

The collaborative mind mapping approach is used to assist the conceptualization of the collaborating students and the knowledge transfer between the peers. Possible application scenarios for education have been formulated and evaluated. These scenarios were set in the context of university-level computer science education.

The application of mind-maps in technology-enhanced learning is based on the concept of visualization of knowledge. In the collaborative setting, this visualization is applied to form a common understanding of a topic, develop a set of concepts and relations for a topic, and, as previously mentioned, to assist the transfer of knowledge.

10.1.4   Social Media applied for Self Reflection and Community Feedback

A collaborative peer review system has been applied to the context of university programming lectures as a sample application. PRC is based on the concept of code annotation and assessment. Moreover, the authors of the original code assess the quality of reviews, and discussion of the reviews and assessments is possible and encouraged.

This approach is based on fundamental concepts of cognitivism, where reflection, abstraction and meta-cognition are consider core parts of the learning process. This reflection and self-reflection based approach is socially enhanced by the integration of communication and discussion into the material created by the peer students. Educators are assisted with statements on the quality of the reviews. The reliability of these statements has been shown in an evaluation by students from various computer-science related curricula.

10.1.5   Social Media in Collaborative, Mobile Learning

Within the scenario of a field-trip supporting solution, TUGeoWiki has successfully been developed. This geospatially enhanced wiki system is based on the concept of every entry being geospatially identified and thus matching the concept of a *place*. Mobile applications for various platforms have been developed.

Educational application of this software is based on a constructivist learning theory approach of collaborative authoring. This collaborative authoring is supported by the possibility of just-in-time sharing of resources and the geospatial localization of all contents and images. Educators are assisted with the traceability of the individual students' participation in the collaborative process.

A set of possible application scenarios has been identified and analyzed. These scenarios were successfully tested with small groups of participants. Future development of an application outside technology-enhanced learning in the context of archeology and medicine is also aimed at.

10.2 Conclusions

Technology-enhanced learning has become a fundamental part of higher education in the recent years. It is used to support both students and lecturers in the process of learning and teaching. Due to the evolution of technology-enhanced learning from early CBT and WBT, this support has, for a long time, been mainly focused on the support of formal aspects, based on predefined structures and pre-assembled learning material.

One of the aspects which has previously received less attention is informal learning. Informal learning is that part of the learning process, which occurs outside lectures and structures, and plays an important role in the consolidation of knowledge.

Contemporaneously to this development in education, social and user-driven approaches have gained importance in the Web – a development, which has been summarized under the term Web 2.0. One of the aspects of this development is the rising importance of social media. This term describes applications used for the creation of content by users for and in communities of interest, learning or practice.

These applications are characterized by participation, openness, conversation, connectedness and sense of communality. The foundations of social media are communication, collaboration and sharing.

In the context of technology-enhanced learning, the application of social media to facilitate informal learning has been proposed. A set of specific scenarios for the inclusion of distinct social media applications to the context of higher education has been developed, implemented and evaluated.

Social Media can be a useful addition to the portfolio of technology-enhanced learning, although the didactical approach should not be solemnly based on their application. However, they can be used to facilitate the learning progress by encouraging informal learning, supporting reflection, and fostering communication and collaboration.

Appendix A.: List of Figures

Appendix B.:   List of Tables

Appendix C.: References

Alavi, M. (1994). Computer-Mediated Collaborative Learning: An Empirical Evaluation. *MIS Quaterly* 18(2), 159-174.

Alexander, B. (2006). Web 2.0: A New Wave of Innovation for Teaching and Learning? *EDUCAUSE Review* 41(2), 32-44.

Allen, I. and Seaman, J. (2004). *Entering the Mainstream: The Quality and Extent of Online Education in the United States, 2003 and 2004*. Needham, MA, USA. 0-9677741-8-7

Alspaugh, T. A. and Antón, A. I. (2008). Scenario support for effective requirements. *Information and Software Technology* 50(3), 198-220.

Anderson, N. (2006). *Tim Berners-Lee on Web 2.0: "nobody even knows what it means"* Retrieved 2009-07-06, from http://arstechnica.com/news.ars/post/20060901-7650.html

Anderson, P. (2007). *What is Web 2.0? Ideas, technologies and implications for education* Retrieved 2009-07-10, from http://www.jisc.ac.uk/media/documents/techwatch/tsw0701b.pdf.

Anido, L. (2006). An observatory for e-learning technology standards. *Advanced Technology for Learning* 3(2), 99-108.

Autonomy Inc. (2007). *Autonomy Technical Overview* Retrieved 2008-12-10, from http://www.autonomy.com/content/Technology/index.en.html.

Bächle, M. (2005). Virtuelle Communities als Basis für ein erfolgreiches Wissensmanagement. *HMD - Praxis der Wirtschaftsinformatik*(246)

Bächle, M. (2006). Social Software. *Informatik-Spektrum* 29(2), 121-124.

Baird, D. E. and Fisher, M. (2006). Neomillennial user experience design strategies: Utilizing social networking media to support "always on" learning styles. *Journal of Educational Technology Systems* 34(1), 5-32.

Baker, J. H. (2003). The learning log. *Journal of Information Systems in Education* 14(1), 11-13.

Bettag, U. (2001). Web-Services. *Informatik-Spektrum* 24(5), 302-304.

Bibliographisches Institut (2005). Brockhaus Multimedial. Mannheim. 978-3-411-06726-8, Retrieved Access Date, from http://www.brockhaus-multimedial.de/, 2009-04-03

Bibliographisches Institut (2009). *Brockhaus Enzyklopädie*. Mannheim. 978-3-7653-4140-3

Boyd, D. M. and Ellison, N. B. (2007). Social Network Sites: Definition, History, and Scholarship *Journal of Computer-Mediated Communication* 13(1)

Brandes, U., Eiglsperger, M., Herman, I., Himsolt, M. and Marshall, M. S. (2002). *GraphML Progress Report: Structural Layer Proposal. 9th International Symposium on Graph Drawing* Springer-Verlag. 501-510.

Bransford, J. D., Brown, A. L. and Cocking, R. R., Eds. (2002). How People Learn: Brain, Mind, Experience, and School. Expanded Edition, National Academies Press.

Brohn, D. (1983). Academic priorities in structural engineering - the importance of a visual schema. *The Structural Engineer* 61 A(1), 13-16.

Bush, V. (1945). As We May Think. *The Atlantic Monthly* 176, 202-208.

Buzan, T. (1976). *Use Both Sides of Your Brain*. 978-0525474364

Buzan, T. and Buzan, B. (2006). *The Mind-Map Book*, Random House UK. 978-1406610208

Carroll, J. M. and Mack, R. L. (1999). Metaphor, computing systems, and active learning. *International Journal of Human-Computer Studies* 51(2), 385-403.

Carroll, J. M., Rosson, M. B., George Chin, J., J\, \#252 and Koenemann, r. (1998). Requirements Development in Scenario-Based Design. *IEEE Trans. Softw. Eng.* 24(12), 1156-1170.

Chen, N. S., Lin, K. M. and Kinshuk (2008). Analysing users' satisfaction with e-learning using a negative critical incidents approach. *Innovations in Education and Teaching International* 45(2), 115-126.

Chen, X. and Shi, S. (2009). A Literature Review of Privacy Research on Social Network Sites. *Proceedings of the 2009 International Conference on Multimedia Information Networking and Security - Volume 01*, IEEE Computer Society.

Cohen, E. and Krishnamurthy, B., A (2006). A short walk in the Blogistan. *Computer Networks: The International Journal of Computer and Telecommunications Networking* 50(5), 615-630.

Coyle, F. P. (2002). XML, web services and the changing face of distributed computing. *Ubiquity* 3(10), 2.

Cunningham, W. (2005). *Correspondence on the Etymology of a Wiki* Retrieved 2009-11-19, from http://c2.com/doc/etymology.html.

Denning, T., Kelly, M., Lindquist, D., Malani, R., Griswold, W. G. and Simon, B. (2007). Lightweight preliminary peer review: does in-class review make sense? *38th SIGCSE Technical Symposium on Computer Science Education,* Covington, Kentucky, United States, SIGCSE. 266-270.

Dösinger, G., Maurer, L. and Tochtermann, K. (2007). How users behave in a combined community/content environment. *ICL 2007,* Villach, Austria.

Douglis, F. (2010). It's All About the (Social) Network. *IEEE Internet Computing* 14(1), 4-6.

Downes, S. (2005). E-learning 2.0. *ACM eLearn Magazine*

Du, H. and Wagner, C. (2005). Learning with Weblogs: An Empirical Investigation. *38th Annual Hawaii International Conference on System Sciences (HICSS '05).*

Du, H. and Wagner, C. (2006). Weblog success: Exploring the role of technology. *International Journal of Human-Computer Studies* 64(9), 789-798.

Du, H. and Wagner, C. (2007). Learning With Weblogs: Enhancing Cognitie and Social Knowledge Construction. *IEEE Transactions on Professional Communication* 50(1), 1-16.

Duffy, P. and Bruns, A. (2006). The Use of Blogs, Wikis and RSS in Education: A Conversation of Possibilities. *Online Learning and Teaching Conference,* Brisbane. 31-38.

Ebner, M. (2007). E-Learning 2.0 = E-Learning 1.0 + Web 2.0. *2nd international conference on Availability, Reliability and Security.* 1235-1239.

Ebner, M., Dorfinger, J., Neuper, W. and Safran, C. (2009). First Experiences with OLPC in European Classrooms. *World Conference on E-Learning in Corporate, Government, Healthcare, & Higher Education,* Vancouver, Canada, AACE. 1226-1234.

Ebner, M., Kickmeier-Rust, M. D. and Holzinger, A. (2008). Utilizing Wiki-Systems in higher education classes: a chance for universal access? *Universal Access in the Information Society.* Heidelberg, Berlin, New York, Springer

Ebner, M. and Maurer, H. (2007). Blogging in Higher Education. *World Conference on E-Learning in Corporate, Government, Healthcare, and Higher Education,* Québec, Canada. 767-774.

Ebner, M., Nagler, W. and Saranti, A. (2007). TU Graz goes Podcast. *3rd International Microlearning Conference.* 221-233.

Ebner, M., Scerbakov, N. and Maurer, H. (2006a). New Features for eLearning in Higher Education for Civil Engineering. *Journal of Universal Computer Science* 0(0), 93-106.

Ebner, M. and Schiefner, M. (2008). Microblogging - more than fun? *IADIS Mobile Learning Conference 2008.* 155-159.

Ebner, M. and Walder, U. (2007). e-Learning in Civil Engineering - Six Years of Experience at Graz University of Technology. *24th W78 Conference,* Maribor, Slovenia. 749-754.

Ebner, M. and Walder, U. (2008). E-Education in Civil Engineering - A Promise for the Future? *6th AECEF Symposium Education in Changing Europe,* Vilnius, Lituania. 16-26.

Ebner, M., Zechner, J. and Holzinger, A. (2006b). Why is Wikipedia so Successful? Experiences in Establishing the Principles in Higher Education. *6th International Conference on Knowledge Management (I-Know'06),* Graz, Austria. 527-535.

EduTools. (2009). *EduTools Homepage* Retrieved 2009-05-12, from http://www.edutools.info/index.jsp?pj=1.

Efimova, L. and Fiedler, S. (2004). Learnign Webs: Learning in Weblog Networks. *IADIS International Cnference Web Based Communities,* Lisbon, Portugal.

Eppler, M. (2006). A comparison between concept maps, mind maps, conceptual diagrams, and visual metaphors as complementary tools for knowledge construction and sharing *Information Visualization* 5(3), 202-210.

Fallows, S. and Chandramohan, B. (2001). Multiple Approaches to Assessment: reflections on use of tutor, peer and self assesment. *Teaching in Higher Education* 6(2), 229-246.

Farrand, P., Hussain, F. and Hennessy, E. (2002). The efficacy of the `mind map' study technique. *MEDICAL EDUCATION* 36(5), 426-431.

Fruchtermann, T. M. and Reingold, E. M. (1991). Graph drawing by force-directed placement. *Software-Practice & Experience* 21(11), 1129-1164.

Fucks-Kittowski, F., Köhler, A. and Fuhr, D. (2004). Roughing up Processes the wiki Way - Knowlede Communities in the Context of Work and Learning Processes. *I-Know 2004*. 484-493.

Garcia-Barrios, V. and Safran, C. (2009). What Students Really Need beyond Learning Content: Ubiquitous Shared-connectivity Services to Foster Learning Communities on the Campus. *MindTrek 2009 Conference,* Tampere, Finland, ACM.

Garcia-Barrios, V. M., Hemmelmayr, A. and Leitner, H. (2009). Personalized Systems Need Adaptable Privacy Statements! How to Make Privacy-related Legal Aspects Usable and Retraceable. *Proceedings of the 2009 Second International Conference on Advances in Human-Oriented and Personalized Mechanisms, Technologies, and Services*, IEEE Computer Society.

Gehringer, E. F. (2001). Electronic peer review and peer grading in computer-science courses. *32nd SIGCSE Symposium on Computer Science Education,* Charlotte, North Carolina, SIGCSE. 139-143.

Geoghengan, M. W. and Klass, D. (2005). *Podcast Solutions: The Complete Guide to Podcasting*, friends of ED. 978-1590595541

Gillmor, D. (2004). *We the Media. Grassroots Journalism by the People, for the People*, O'Reilly Media. 0596007337

Graf, S., Lin, T. and Kinshuk, J. (2008). The relationship between learning styles and cognitive traits - Getting additional information for improving student modelling. *Computers in Human Behavior* 24(2), 122-137.

Granitzer, G., Stocker, A., Hoefler, P. and Tochtermann, K. (2008). Informal Learning with Semantic Wikis in Enterprises. *World Conference on Educational Multimedia, Hypermedia and Telecommunication (ED-MEDIA)*, AACE. 6165-6170.

Green, K. C. (2006). *The 2006 Campus Computing Survey*, The Campus Computing Project.

Green, K. C. (2007). *The 2007 Campus Computing Survey*, The Campus Computing Project.

Griswold, W. G. (2007). Five enablers for Mobile 2.0. *Computer* 40(10), 96-98.

Gross, R., Acquisti, A. and H. John Heinz, I. (2005). Information revelation and privacy in online social networks. *Proceedings of the 2005 ACM workshop on Privacy in the electronic society*, Alexandria, VA, USA, ACM.

Grossman, L. (2006). Time's person of the Year: You. *Time*(168), 38-41.

Gütl, C. (2008). Moving Towards a Generic, Service-based Architecture for Flexible Teaching and Learning Activities. *Architecture Solutions for E-Learning Systems*. Pahl, C., Idea Group Inc.

Gütl, C. and Safran, C. (2006). Personalized Access to Meeting Records for the Knowledge Transfer and Learning Purposes in Companies. *International Conference on Multimedia and information and Communication Technologies in Education (mICTE),* Sevilla, Spain. 1052-1056.

Heidemann, J. (2009). Online Social Networks – Ein sozialer und technischer Überblick. *Informatik-Spektrum*

Helic, D. (2005). An Ontology-Based Approach to Supporting Didactics in E-Learning Systems. *Proceedings of the Fifth IEEE International Conference on Advanced Learning Technologies*, IEEE Computer Society.

Helic, D. (2007). Formal Representations of Learning Scenarios. *Journal of Universal Computer Science* 13(4), 504-531.

Helic, D., Krottmaier, H., Maurer, H. and Scerbakov, N. (2005). Enabling Project-Based Learning in WBT Systems. *International Journal on E-Learning* 4(4), 445-461.

Helic, D., Maurer, H. and Scerbakov, N. (2004a). Discussion Forums as Learning Ressources in Wbe-Based Education. *Advanced Technology for Learning* 1(1), 8-15.

Helic, D., Maurer, H. and Scerbakov, N. (2004b). Discussion Forums as Learning Ressources in Web-Based Education. *Advanced technology for learning* 1(1), 8-15.

Helic, D., Maurer, H. and Scerbakov, N. (2004c). Knowledge Transfer Processes in a Modern WBT System. *Journal of Network and Computer Applications* 27(3), 163-190.

Hill, W. C., Hollan, J. D., Wroblewski, D. and McCandless, T. (1992). Edit wear and read wear. *Proceedings of the SIGCHI conference on Human factors in computing systems,* Monterey, California, United States, ACM.

Hiranabe, K. (2007). *Agile Modeling With Mind Map and UML* Retrieved 2008-03-02, from http://whitepapers.techrepublic.com.com/abstract.aspx?docid=397033.

Holzinger, A. (1997). Computer-aided Mathematics Instruction with Mathematica 3.0. *Mathematica in Education and Research* 6(4), 37-40.

Holzinger, A. (2002). *Multimedia Basics, Volume 2: Learning. Cognitive Fundamentals of multimedial Information Systems (www.basiswissen-multimedia.at)*. New Delhi, Laxmi.

Holzinger, A., Kickmeier-Rust, M. D. and Albert, D. (2008). Dynamic Media in Computer Science Education; Econtent Complexity and Learning Performance: Is Less More? *Educational Technology & Society* 11(1), 279-290.

Hyperwave. (2009). *Hyperwave Information Server* Retrieved 2009-02-22, from http://www.hyperwave.com.

Illich, I. (1971). *Deschooling Society*, Marion Boyars Publishers, Ltd. 0714508799

Jackson, C. and Wang, H. J. (2007). Subspace: secure cross-domain communication for web mashups. *Proceedings of the 16th international conference on World Wide Web,* Banff, Alberta, Canada, ACM.

Japan Electronics an Information Technology Industries Association. (2002). *Exchangable image file format for digital still cameras: Exif version 2.2*, from http://www.exif.org/Exif2-2.PDF.

Java, A., Song, X., Finin, T. and Tseng, B. (2007). Why we twitter: understanding microblogging usage and communities. *9th WebKDD and 1st SNA-KDD 2007 workshop on Web mining and social network analysis,* San Jose, California, ACM. 56-65.

Jensen, J. F. (2008). The concept of interactivity -- revisited: four new typologies for a new media landscape. *Proceeding of the 1st international conference on Designing interactive user experiences for TV and video,* Silicon Valley, California, USA, ACM.

Johansen, R. (1988). *GroupWare: Computer Support for Business Teams*, The Free Press. 0029164915

Johnson, R. T. and Johnson, D. W. (1994). An overview of cooporative learning. *Creativity and Collaborative Learning: The Practical Guide to Empowering Students and Teachers.* Thousands, J., Villa, R. and Nevin, A. Baltimore, Brookes Press, 31-44.

Jonassen, D. H. (1992). Semantic Networking as Cognitive Tools. *Cognitive Tools for Learning.* Kommers, P. A. M., Jonassen, D. H. and Mayes, J. T., Springer-Verlag New York, Inc., 12-22.

Jonassen, D. H. (2001). Semantic Networking as Cognitive Tools. *Cognitive Tools for Learning.* Kommers, P. A. M., Jonassen, D. H. and Mayes, J. T., Springer-Verlag New York, Inc., 12-22.

Jones, R. (2009). *Social Media Marketing 101, Part 1* Retrieved 2009-08-24, from http://sbinfocanada.about.com/gi/dynamic/offsite.htm?zi=1/XJ&sdn=sbinfocanada&cdn=money&t m=49&f=00&tt=8&bt=1&bts=1&zu=http%3A//searchenginewatch.com/3632809.

Kali, Y. and Ronen, M. (2005). Design principles for online peer-evaluation: fostering objectivity. *2005 Conference on Computer Support for Collaborative Learning: Learning 2005: the Next 10 Years!,* Taipei, Taiwan, International Society of the Learning Sciences. 247-251.

Kinshuk and Sampson, D. G. (2004). Special issue on cognition and exploratory learning in the diital age. *Innovations in Education and Teaching International* 43(2), 105-108.

Koch, M., Richter, A. and Schlosser, A. (2007). Produkte zum IT-gestützten Social Networking in Unternehmen. *Wirtschaftsinformatik* 49(6), 233-253.

Kolbitsch, J. and Maurer, H. (2005). Community Building around Encyclopaedic Knowledge. *Journal of Computing and Information Technology* 14(3), 175-190.

Kolbitsch, J., Safran, C. and Maurer, H. (2007). Dynamic Adaption of Content and Structure in Electronic Encyclopaedias. *Journal of Digital Information* 8, electronic publications.

Koper, R. and Olivier, B. (2004). Representing the learning design of units of learning. *Educational Technology & Society* 7(3), 97-111.

Kosorukoff, A. (2001). Human-based Genetic Algrithm. *IEEE Transactions on Systems, Man, and Cybernetics,* 3464-3469.

Kravcik, M., Specht, M., Kaibel, A. and Terrenghi, L. (2003). *Collecting data on field trips - RAFT approach.* The 3rd IEEE International Conference on Advanced Learning Technologies. 478.

Kritikopoulos, A., Sideri, M. and Varlamis, I. (2006). *BlogRank: ranking weblogs based on connectivity and similarity features. 2nd international Workshop on Advanced Architectures and Algorithms For internet Delivery and Applications* 8.

Kruitbosch, G. and Nack, F. (2008). Broadcast yourself on YouTube: really? *Proceeding of the 3rd ACM international workshop on Human-centered computing,* Vancouver, British Columbia, Canada, ACM.

Kumar, R., Novak, J., Raghavan, P. and Tomkins, A. (2004). Structure and Evolution of Blogspace. *Communications of the ACM* 47(12), 35-39.

Kunow, K. and Schwickert, A. C. (1999). *Intranet-basiertes Workgroup Computing*, Justus-Liebig-Universität Giessen.

LaQuey, T. L. (1990). *The user's directory of computer networks*, Digital Press. 1-55558-047-5

Leidner, D. and Jarvenpaa, S. (1995). The use of information technology to enhacne management school education: a theoretical view. *MIS Quaterly* 19(3), 265-291.

Leskovec, J. and Horvitz, E. (2008). Planetary-scale views on a large instant-messaging network. *Proceeding of the 17th international conference on World Wide Web,* Beijing, China, ACM.

Leuf, B. and Cunningham, W. (2001). *The wiki Way. Quick Collaboration on the Web*, Addison-Wesley.

Li, B., Xu, S. and Zhang, J. (2007). *Enhancing clustering weblog documents by utilizing author/reader comments.* 45th Annual Southeast Regional Conference. 94-99.

Lipson, H. (2008). Evolutionary synthesis of kinematic mechanisms. *Artif. Intell. Eng. Des. Anal. Manuf.* 22(3), 195-205.

Lonsdale, P., Baber, C. and Sharples, M. (2004). A Context Awareness Architecture for Facilitating Mobile Learning. *Learning with Mobile Devices: Research and Development.* Attewell, J. and Savill-Smith, C. London, Learning and Skills Development Agency, 79-85.

MacKay, D. J. C. (2003). *Information Theory, Inference, and Learning Algorithms*, Cambridge University Press. 978-0521642989

Martin, C. J. (2007). Scribbles: an exploratory study of sketch based support for early collaborative object oriented design. *12th annual SIGCSE conference on Innovation and technology in computer science education,* Dundee, Scotland, ACM.

Maurer, H. and Safran, C. (2007). Beyond Wikipedia. *World Conference on Educational Multimedia, Hypermedia and Telecommunications (ED-Media).* 4444-4450.

Mayfield, A. (2008). *What is Social Media? An eBook from iCrossing* Retrieved 2009-07-06, from http://www.icrossing.co.uk/fileadmin/uploads/eBooks/What_is_Social_Media_iCrossing_ebook.pdf.

McMartin, F., Wetzel, M. and Hanleym, G. (2004). Ensirung Quality in Peer Review. *2004 Joint ACM/IEEE Conference on Digital Libraries,* Long Beach, California, United States. 392.

Mediawiki. (2008a). *Help:Templates* Retrieved 2009-03-24, from http://www.mediawiki.org/w/index.php?title=Help:Templates&oldid=163132.

Mediawiki. (2008b). *Manual:Special pages* Retrieved 2009-03-24, from http://www.mediawiki.org/w/index.php?title=Manual:Special_pages&oldid=171875.

Mento, A. J., Martinelli, P. and Jones, R. M. (1999). Mind Mapping in Executive Education: Applications and Outcomes. *The Journal of Management Development* 18(4), 390-407.

Merriam-Webster. (2009). *Merriam-Webster's Online Dictionary* Retrieved 2009-07-06, from http://www.merriam-webster.com/dictionary.

Mifsud, L. (2002). *Alternative Learning Arenas - Pedagogical Challenges to Mobile Learning Technology in Education*. IEEE International Workshop on Wireless and Mobile Technologies in Education (WMTE'02), Växjö, Sweden. 112-117.

Milgram, S. (1967). The small world problem. *Psychology Today* 2(1), 60-67.

Millen, D., Feinberg, J. and Kerr, B. (2005). Social bookmarking in the enterprise. *Queue* 3(9), 28-35.

Millen, D. R., Feinberg, J. and Kerr, B. (2006). Dogear: Social bookmarking in the enterprise. *Proceedings of the SIGCHI conference on Human Factors in computing systems,* Montr\&\#233;al, Qu\&\#233;bec, Canada, ACM.

Mioduser, D., Nachmias, R., Oren, A. and Lahav, O. (1999). Web-based learning environments (WBLE): Current implementation and evolving trends. *Journal of Network and Computer Applications* 22(4), 233-247.

Möller, E. (2006). *Die heimliche Medienrevolution*. Hannover, Germany, Heise Zeitschriften Verlag Gmbh & Co KG. 3-936931-36-4

Nardi, B. A., Schiano, D. J., Gumbrecht, M. and Swartz, L. (2004). Why we blog. *Commun. ACM* 47(12), 41-46.

Neal, L. (2007). Predictions for 2007. *ACM eLearn Magazine* 42(1)

Nielsen (2009). *Global Faces and Networked Places*.

Nielsen, J. and Mack, R. L., Eds. (1994). Usability Inspection Methods, Wiley.

Norris, C. and Soloway, E. (2004). Envisioning the Handheld-Centric Classroom. *Journal of Educational Computing Research* 30(4), 281-294.

Notess, M. (2009). Not Dead Yet: Why the Institutional LMS is Worth Saving. *eLearn* 2009(7)

O'Reilly, T. (2005). *What Is Web 2.0 - Design Patterns and Business Models for the Next Generation of Software* Retrieved 2010-03-17, from http://www.oreillynet.com/pub/a/oreilly/tim/news/2005/09/30/what-is-web-20.html.

Oblinger, D. G. and Oblinger, J. L., Eds. (2005). Educatiiong the Net Generation, EDUCAUSE.

Ocker, R. (2001). Collaborative Learning Environments: Exploring Student Attitudes and Satisfaction in Face-to-Face and Asynchronous Computer Conferencing Settings. *Journal of Interactive Learning Research* 12(4), 427-448.

OECD Publishing, Ed. (2006). Think Scenarios, Rethink Education: Schooling for Tomorrow, Organisation for Economic Co-operation and Development.

Page, L., Brin, S., Motwani, R. and Winograd, T. (1999). *The pagerank citation ranking: Bringing order to the web.*, Stanford, USA.

Paquet, S. (2003). *Personal knowledge publishing and is uses in research* Retrieved 2009-04-03, from http://www.knowledgeboard.com/item/253.

Poller, A. (2008). *Privatsphärenschutz in Soziale-Netzwerke-Plattformen*. Darmstadt, Germany, Fraunhofer-Intitut für Sichere Informationstechnologie.

Presse, D. (2006). *Alexander: Wikipedia-Alternative aus Graz*   Retrieved 2009-02-22, from http://diepresse.com/home/techscience/internet/82338/index.do?from=suche.intern.portal.

Presse, D. (2009). *Die Presse*   Retrieved 2009-02-22, from http://diepresse.at/.

Priedhorsky, R., Jordan, B. and Terveen, L. (2007). How a personalized geowiki can help bicyclists share information more effectively. *2007 International Symposium in Wikis (WikiSym)*. 93-98.

Raitman, R. and Augar, N. (2005). Employing Wikis for Online Collaboration in the E-Learning Environment: Case Study. *Third international Conference on information Technology and Applications (Icita'05)*, IEEE Computer Society. 142-146.

Ramsay, W. and Ransley, W. (1986). A method of analysis for determining dimensions of teaching style. *Teaching and Teacher Education* 2(1), 69-79.

Razavi, M. N. and Iverson, L. (2006). A grounded theory of information sharing behavior in a personal learning space. *20th Anniversary Conference on Computer Supported Coorporative Work (CSCW '06)*. 459-468.

Reinhardt, W., Ebner, M., Beham, G. and Costa, C. (2009). How People are Using Twitter during Conferences. *5th EduMedia conference,* Salzbrug, Austria. 145-156.

Richardson, W. (2006). *Blogs, wikis, podcasts, and other powerful web tools for classrooms*. Thousand Oaks, CA, Corwin Press.

Riding, R. J. (1997). On the Nature of Cognitive Style. *Educational Psychology* 17(1-2), 29-49.

Safran, C. (2008a). Blogging in Higher Education Programming Lectures: An Empirical Study. *ACM Mindtrek '08,* Tampere, Finland, ACM.

Safran, C. (2008b). Collaborative Feedback: Code Peer Review in Higher Education. *International Conference on Interactive Computer aided Learning (ICL)* Villach, Austria, kassel university press. electronic publication.

Safran, C. (2009a). Application Scenarios for Collaborative Online Mind Maps in Higher Education. *International Conference on Interactive Computer Aided Learning (ICL)* Villach, Austria, kassel university press. electronic publication.

Safran, C. (2009b). Code Peer Review in Higher Education: Evaluating the Application for Programming Lectures. *International Conference on Interactive Computer Aided Learning (ICL)* Villach, Austria, kassel university press. electronic publication.

Safran, C., Ebner, M., Garcia-Barrios, V. and Kappe, F. (2009a). Higher Education m-Learning and e-Learning Scenarios for a Geospatial Wiki. *World Conference on E-Learning in Corporate, Government, Healthcare, & Higher Education,* Vancouver, Canada, AACE. 3678-3685.

Safran, C., Ebner, M., Kappe, F. and Holzinger, A. (2009b). m-Learning in the Field: A Mobile Geospatial Wiki as an example for Geo-Tagging in Civil Engineering Education. *Looking Toward the Future of Technology-Enhanced Education: Ubiquitous Learning and the Digital Native*. Ebner, M. and Schaffert, S., Information Science Pub, 444-454.

Safran, C., Garcia-Barrios, V. and Ebner, M. (2009c). The Benefits of Geo-Tagging and Microblogging in m-Learning: a Use Case. *MindTrek 2009 Conference,* Tampere, Finland, ACM.

Safran, C., Garcia-Barrios, V. and Gütl, C. (2006). A Concept-based Context Modelling System for the Support of Teaching and Learning Activities. *Society for Information Technology and Teacher Education International Conference.* 2395-2402.

Safran, C., Gütl, C. and Helic, D. (2007a). The Impact of Web 2.0 on Learning at a Technical University - A usage survey. *World Conference on E-Learning in Coporate, Government, Healthcare, and Higher Education (E-Learn).* 436-443.

Safran, C., Helic, D. and Gütl, C. (2007b). E-Learning practices and Web 2.0. *International Conference in Interactive Computer Aided Learning,* Villach, Austria.

Safran, C. and Kappe, F. (2007). Quantitative Analysis of Success Factors for User Generated Content. *International Conference on New Media Technology (I-MEDIA),* Graz. 65-72.

Safran, C. and Kappe, F. (2008). Success Factors in a Weblog Community. *Journal of Universal Computer Science* 14(4), 546-556.

Safran, C. and Zaka, B. (2008). A geospatial Wiki for m-Learning. *International Conference on Computer Science and Software Engineering* Wuhan, China, IEEE Computer Society. 109-112.

Schaffert, S. (2006). Semantic Social Software: Semantically enabled Social Software or Socially enabled Semantic Web. *Semantic Systems. From Visions to Applications.* Schaffert, S. and Sure, Y. Vienna, Austria, OCG Verlag

Schmees, M. (2006). Organizing technology enhanced learning. *Proceedings of the 8th international conference on Electronic commerce: The new e-commerce: innovations for conquering current barriers, obstacles and limitations to conducting successful business on the internet,* Fredericton, New Brunswick, Canada, ACM.

Shapiro, C. and Varian, H. R. (1999). *Information Rules,* Harvard Business Press. 087584863X

Sharples, M. (2000). The design of personal mobile technologies for lifelong learning. *Computers & Education* 34, 177-193.

Sharples, M., Corlett, D. and Westmancott, O. (2002). The Design and Implementation of a Mobile Learning Resource. *Personal and Ubiquitous Computing* 6(3), 220-234.

Sitthiworachart, J. and Joy, M. (2004a). Effective peer assessment for learning computer programming. *9th Annual SigCSE Converence on Innovation and Technology in Computer Science Education,* Leeds, United Kingdom, ITiCSE. 122-126.

Sitthiworachart, J. and Joy, M. (2004b). Web-based peer assessmet system with anonymous communication tool. *IEEE Conference on Advanced Learning Technologies.* 918-919.

Six Apart. (2004). *Trackback Technical Specification* Retrieved 2008-10-12, from http://www.sixapart.com/pronet/docs/trackback_spec.

Specht, M., Kaibel, A. and Apelt, S. (2005). *Extending LCMS for remote accessible field trips in RAFT.* Third IEEE International Conference on Pervasive Computing and Communications Workshops. 302-306.

Staddon, J. (2009). Finding "hidden" connections on linkedIn an argument for more pragmatic social network privacy. *Proceedings of the 2nd ACM workshop on Security and artificial intelligence*, Chicago, Illinois, USA, ACM.

Stanley, G. (2004). Introducing your students to Blogs. *IATEFL Issues* April-May, 178.

Strijker, A. and Collis, B. (2002). New Pedagogies and Re-Usable Learning Objects: Toward a Different Role for an LMS. *World Conference on Educational Multimedia, Hypermedia and Telecommunications*. 334-339.

Strouhal, L. (2009). *Mind-Mapping - A collaborative web-based approach*. Institute for Information Systems and Computer Media. Graz, Graz University of Technology. **MSc.**

Sullivan, S. (1994). Reciprocal Peer Reviews. *25th SIGCSE Symposium on Computer Science Education,* Phoenix, Arizona, SIGSCE. 314-318.

Tatar, D., Roschelle, J., Vahey, P. and Penuel, W. R. (2003). Handhelds Go to School: Lessons Learned. *Computer* 36(9), 30-37.

Templeton, M. (2008). *Microblogging Defined* Retrieved 2009-05-25, from http://microblink.com/2008/11/11/microblogging-defined/.

Tochermann, K. and Granitzer, G. (2008). The Long Way towards Workplace-Integrated Learning. *Proceedings of the 2008 Eighth IEEE International Conference on Advanced Learning Technologies*, IEEE Computer Society.

Tochtermann, K. and Schwartz, S. (2000). *Enhancing Information Portals with Internet-based GIS*. WebNet World Conference on the WWW and Internet 2000, San Antonio, Texas, AACE. 530-536.

Trahasch, S. (2004). From peer assessment towards collaborative learning. *34th Conference on frontiers in education*. 16-20.

Tretiakov, A. and Kinshuk (2008). Towards designing m-learning systems for maximal likelihood of acceptance. *International Journal of Engineering Education* 24(1), 79-83.

Trytten, D. A. (2005). A Design for Team Peer Code Review. *36th SIGCSE technical symposium in Computer science education*. 455-459.

Van der Heijden, K. (1997). Scenarios, Strategy, and the Strategy Process. *presearch* 1(1)

Voelkel, M. and Oren, E. (2006). Towards a Wiki Interchange Format (WIF). *First Workshop on Semantic Wikis -- From Wiki To Semantics*.

Voss, J. (2005). Measuring Wikipedia. *10th ISSI Conference,* Stockholm.

W3C Working Group. (2004). *Web Services Glossary* Retrieved 2009-08-27, from http://www.w3.org/TR/ws-gloss/.

Watt, S. E., Lea, M. and Spears, R. (2002). How Social is Internet Communication? A Reappraisal of Bandwidth and Anonymity Effects. *Virtual society? Technology, cyberhole, reality.* Woolgar, S. Oxford, UK, Oxford University Press, 61-77.

Weideman, M. and Kritzinger, W. (2003) "Concept Mapping - a proposed theoretical model for the implementation as a knowledge repository." Working paper from the "ICT in Higher Education" research project.

White, D. (2007). *Results of the 'Online Tools Use Survey' undertaken by the JISC funden SPIRE project.* Retrieved 2009-03-04, from http://tallblog.conted.ox.ac.uk/wp-content/uploads/2007/03/survey-summary.pdf.

Wikipedia. (2008). *WikiProject Geographical coordinates* Retrieved 2009-03-04, from http://en.wikipedia.org/w/index.php?title=Wikipedia:WikiProject_Geographical_coordinates&oldid=174960235.

Willis, C. L. and Miertschin, S. L. (2005). Mind tools for enhancing thinking and learning skills. *6th conference on Information technology education,* Newark, NJ, USA, ACM.

Willis, C. L. and Miertschin, S. L. (2006). Mind maps as active learning tools. *J. Comput. Small Coll.* 21(4), 266-272.

Wiltse, E. M. (2004). Blog, Blog, Blog: Experiences with web logs in journalism classes. *Internationa Symposium on Online Journalism.*

Xiaosong, L. (2006). Using Peer Review to Assess Coding Standards - A Case Study. *36th Annual Conference on Frontiers in Education.* 9-14.

Yanbe, Y., Jatowt, A., Nakamura, S. and Tanaka, K. (2007). Can social bookmarking enhance search in the web? *Proceedings of the 7th ACM/IEEE-CS joint conference on Digital libraries,* Vancouver, BC, Canada, ACM.

Young, R. M. and Barnard, P. (1987). The use of scenarios in human-computer interaction research: turbocharging the tortoise of cumulative science. *SIGCHI Bull.* 17(SI), 291-296.

Zaka, B. and Safran, C. (2008). Emerging Web Based Learning Systems and Scalability Issues. *Proceedings of the 2008 International Conference on Computer Science and Software Engineering - Volume 05,* IEEE Computer Society.

Zaka, B., Safran, C. and Kappe, F. (2006). A blended learning approach in the news domain. *International Conference on Multimedia and Information and Communication Technologies in Education,* Sevilla, Spain. 1027-1031.

Zaka, B., Safran, C. and Kappe, F. (2007). Personalized Interactive Newscast (PINC): Towards a Multimodal Interface for Personalized News. *International Workshop on Semantic Media Adaption and Personalization.* 56-61.

Zaka, B., Safran, C. and Kappe, F. (2009). Use of similarity detection techniques for adaptive news content delivery and user profiling. *Advances in Semantic Media Adaptation and Personalization, Volume 2.* Angelides, M. C., CRC press, 225 - 246.

Zhao, D. and Rosson, M. B. (2009). How and why people Twitter: the role that micro-blogging plays in informal communication at work. *Proceedings of the ACM 2009 international conference on Supporting group work,* Sanibel Island, Florida, USA, ACM.

Ziewer, P., Ebner, M., Safran, C. and Slany, W. (2007). Searching for Classes of Visual Content in Electronic Lectures. *Proceedings of the Ninth IEEE International Symposium on Multimedia Workshops*, IEEE Computer Society. 377-382.

Appendix D.: Index

www.ingramcontent.com/pod-product-compliance
Lightning Source LLC
Chambersburg PA
CBHW021045210326
41598CB00016B/1102